# MURDER

EDWARD BUTTS

# MURDER

## TWELVE TRUE STORIES OF HOMICIDE IN CANADA

DUNDURN PRESS

TORONTO

Editor: Nicole Chaplin
Design: Jesse Hooper
Printer: Marquis

**Library and Archives Canada Cataloguing in Publication**

Butts, Edward, 1951-
     Murder : twelve true stories of homicide in
Canada / by Edward Butts.

Includes bibliographical references.
Issued also in an electronic format.
ISBN 978-1-55488-762-0

     1. Murder--Canada. I. Title.

HV6535.C3B88 2011          364.152'30971          C2010-902693-4

1   2   3   4   5         15   14   13   12   11

We acknowledge the support of the **Canada Council for the Arts** and the **Ontario Arts Council** for our publishing program. We also acknowledge the financial support of the **Government of Canada** through the **Canada Book Fund** and **Livres Canada Books**, and the **Government of Ontario** through the **Ontario Book Publishers Tax Credit** program, and the **Ontario Media Development Corporation**.

Care has been taken to trace the ownership of copyright material used in this book. The author and the publisher welcome any information enabling them to rectify any references or credits in subsequent editions.

*J. Kirk Howard, President*

Printed and bound in Canada.
www.dundurn.com

| Dundurn Press | Gazelle Book Services Limited | Dundurn Press |
| --- | --- | --- |
| 3 Church Street, Suite 500 | White Cross Mills | 2250 Military Road |
| Toronto, Ontario, Canada | High Town, Lancaster, England | Tonawanda, NY |
| M5E 1M2 | LA1 4XS | U.S.A. 14150 |

*For my grandniece, Capree, born January 14, 2010*

# CONTENTS

# ACKNOWLEDGEMENTS

I would like to thank all of the people at Dundurn Press who were of assistance to me while I was working on this book, especially Michael Carroll and Nicole Chaplin. I would also like to express my gratitude to the following institutions and individuals: Library & Archives Canada, the Royal BC Museum, the Glenbow Institute, the Provincial Archives of Alberta, the Cobourg, Ontario, Public Library, The Beaton Institute of Cape Breton, the Rooms Archives of Newfoundland, Sgt. Douglas Pflug of the Guelph, Ontario, Police Services, Kelly-Ann Turkington, Diane Lamourieux, Ian Kennedy, Melanie Tucker, Susan Kooyman, Katie Roth, Chris Hamilton, John Draper, Anne MacNeil, and as always the staff of the Guelph, Ontario Public Library.

# INTRODUCTION

*Murder is always a mistake.*
*One should never do anything that one cannot talk about after dinner.*
— Oscar Wilde

There is a strong element of pragmatism in Oscar Wilde's famous witticism on the dark subject of murder. Once the foul deed has been committed, it must be cloaked in secrecy to avoid punishment. Even though some countries, like Canada, no longer have capital punishment, there is always the prospect of a long prison term.

Volumes have been written by psychiatrists, criminologists, historians, and numerous experts about why people commit murder. People kill out of greed, jealousy, revenge, and ambition; or to get rid of an inconvenient spouse or relative. Sometimes people kill in blind rage, or while under the influence of alcohol or narcotics. Murder can also happen when another crime, like armed robbery, goes terribly wrong.

People are morbidly fascinated by murder. Murder has been a key element in literature since the biblical story of Cain and Abel. It is also the central theme of *Hamlet* and *Macbeth*, two of Shakespeare's greatest dramas. In the modern age, murder stories have been the bread and butter of the movie and television industries. Some true-life murder stories, like those of Jack the Ripper in England and Lizzie Borden in the United States, have become legendary.

Murder has always haunted Canadian society. Between Confederation in 1867 and the last instance of capital punishment in 1963, more than 700 people convicted of murder were hanged in Canadian jails. This long list of documented executions does not include those from colonial times, nor does it cover convicted murderers whose sentences were commuted or murderers who were never caught. Unfortunately, sometimes murderers get away with it.

Some Canadian murderers acted impulsively. Others cold-heartedly planned their crimes, taking every possible precaution to avoid arrest. Their victims ranged from family members to total strangers. Their bloody deeds made headline news. Then, in typical Canadian fashion, they were forgotten.

No Canadian murder has ever gained such lasting international notoriety as those of the mysterious Ripper or the enigmatic Miss Borden. Even the names Clifford Olsen, Marc Lepine, Paul Bernardo, and Robert Pickton whose brutal multiple homicides shocked and sickened the Canadian people, are not familiar to many people beyond our borders. For that, the majority of Canadians are probably grateful: murder does not enhance the national image.

In London, England, tourists can go on Jack the Ripper tours of Whitechapel, where the killer stalked his human prey. And the Lizzie Borden House in Fall River, Massachusetts, is a bed & breakfast and museum. Tourists to Canada won't find similar attractions to titillate their morbid curiosity, though. At best, there might be a historic plaque marking the site of a noteworthy murder, such as the one on the Gibraltar Point Lighthouse on Toronto Island. And, though there have been a few plays and made-for-TV movies have been based on true Canadian murder cases, there have been no major feature films like *The Boston Strangler* (American, 1968) starring Tony Curtis and Henry Fonda, or *10 Rillington Place* (British, 1971) starring Richard Attenborough and John Hurt. It isn't because Canada doesn't have intriguing, true tales of murder. It does. The following chapters are but a small sampling of homicide in our country before 1950. The crimes they describe were heinous; not at all the sort of thing one could do, and then talk about after dinner.

# 1.

# MURDER AT GIBRALTAR POINT:
## THE LIGHTHOUSE KEEPER

John Paul Radelmüller's death is one of Toronto's oldest murder mysteries. It is well-known among Toronto history buffs that the first keeper of the lighthouse on Toronto Island mysteriously disappeared, allegedly a victim of foul play. But almost nothing has been written about the man himself. In the sketchy accounts that have found their way into print — usually stories based on folklore — he has been described as an unsociable old recluse, a bootlegger who cheated his customers with watered-down booze, and even a traitor and smuggler during the War of 1812. Most of these accounts don't even get his name right: Radmuller, Rademuller, Raddelmullar, and Randan Muller have all appeared in stories. He took the Oath of Allegiance in York (Toronto) on May 5, 1805, and from that record we know that he was a resident of Markham: "Yeoman (farmer) five feet ten inches high blue Eyes & Brown hair Forty two years old."

Thankfully, a series of letters written in Radelmüller's own hand has survived, and they provide a concise autobiography. The letters reveal a man who was reasonably well-educated, polite, humble, and quite public-minded. When Radelmüller arrived in Canada, he'd already lived quite an interesting life as a servant in English royal households.

John Paul Radelmüller was born in 1763 in Anspach, Bavaria. Anspach was the hometown of Princess Wilhelmina Caroline, the wife of England's King George II. England's royal family had been German since 1714 when Queen Anne, the last monarch of the Stuart dynasty, died without an heir. The English crown went to her cousin, George Guelph, the Elector of Hanover. "German George," as his British subjects called him, and his descendants kept close connections with Germany, which included staffing their English homes with German servants. Radelmüller wrote: "In the year 1782, on the 25<sup>th</sup> of Sept.r I had the Honor to become a servant to H.R. Highness the Duke of Gloucester in the Character of Chamber Hussar in which Service and Station I remained till 1798." The term "chamber hussar" indicates that Radelmüller was an attendant in the Duke's bedchamber.

At the time that John Paul Radelmüller became a royal domestic, George III was on the throne and was going mad. His brother, Prince William Henry, Duke of Gloucester, had been banished from Court because he had married a woman of whom the king did not approve. Self-indulgent princes and spoiled princesses must have made life hell for servants like Radelmüller, who bore silent witness to the antics of the dysfunctional family that ruled the most powerful nation in the world. The Duke's son, Prince William Frederick, was an especially obnoxious character whose own royal cousins referred to as "The Contagion." After sixteen years in the Gloucester household, Radelmüller returned to Anspach to take up "farmering."

Radelmüller was happy to see his family and homeland again, but Europe was engulfed in war and revolution. With Anspach sitting directly in the paths of two opposing armies, he decided that his hometown was not a safe place to be.

"As I knowed that I was willcome again where I came from, after some months stay I turn'd a gain to Old England. As it hapened [sic] then H.R. Highness the Duke of Kent Came home from America. I had the Honor soon after his arrival to engage myself with Him as porter."

The Duke of Kent was Prince Edward Augustus, fourth son of King George III, future father of Queen Victoria, and the man for whom Prince Edward Island was named. Edward lived with the knowledge that his father didn't like him. He had extravagant tastes, and kept running up debts that the king had to pay off. The prince was not yet married to the princess who would give birth to Victoria, but was romantically involved with a woman he loved, Alphonse Julie Therese Bernardine de

Montgenet, Baronne de Fortisson de St. Laurent, whom other members of the royal family derisively called "Edward's French Lady." Because her family was *bourgeoisie*, Edward could not marry her.

King George sent Prince Edward on missions all over the Empire, probably to keep him out of England. It was when the prince had returned from Halifax, Nova Scotia, to recuperate from an injury he'd sustained in a fall from a horse, that Radelmüller was taken into his "family" of servants. The king promoted Edward to the rank of general, and made him Commander in Chief of all the British forces in North America. That meant he would soon be sailing back to Halifax, and out of the king's sight.

Thus it was that John Paul Radelmüller found himself en route to the Colonies. The Duke of Gloucester had been an ardent tourist, so Radelmüller was familiar with the task of preparing a royal household for a voyage. "As I was an old travelor," he wrote, "I got charge of the packages."

The "packages" were the prince's personal luggage, and there was a lot of it. Edward always travelled with a large and expensive wardrobe, as well as the very best soldier's equipment. There was also a large amount of furniture, so the prince and his lady love could surround themselves with splendour wherever they went. Having charge of the packages was a huge responsibility, and reflected the confidence the prince had in Radelmüller. Edward and his household sailed from Portsmouth aboard the frigate *Arethusa* on July 25, 1799. Forty-three days later, with cannons and church bells announcing their arrival, they landed at Halifax.

Edward and Alphonse were the guests of Sir John Wentworth, the Governor of Nova Scotia. Servants like Radelmüller would have been fully occupied keeping up with all the social occasions a royal was expected to attend. Nonetheless, Radelmüller took advantage of his days off to explore the countryside. He had not given up his dream of "farmering," and he discovered that he liked Nova Scotia. After only a year in the colony, Edward had to return to England due to poor health. Radelmüller wrote:

"He [Edward] inquired if there were any in His Family that should be desirous to Settle in this Country, and ask'd me if I am one of them. I answered in the affirmative. His R.H.s well knows that I wished to have

Land. He offered me His assistance for some without my asking for any, and [where] I would like to have it if there should be any vacant."

Radelmüller found a parcel of about a thousand acres near Halifax that was available. Prince Edward told Radelmüller that because he had served the royal family faithfully for so many years, he would help him acquire the land. The prince also promised to secure a good job in the Nova Scotia colonial government for Radelmüller because, he said, "it would be a pity to be hid in the Bush."

Radelmüller was overjoyed. Then his plans hit a setback. Just as the prince was about to sail for England, the man he had engaged to replace Radelmüller as his chief servant fell ill. "For which reason H.R.H. desired me to go with him to England and he would give me a free passage out again in the Spring following."

When HMS *Assistance* left Halifax on August 4, 1800, Radelmüller was on board as Edward's porter. He remained in England for another year. Edward recuperated slowly, and Radelmüller felt duty-bound to stay until the prince had fully recovered.

Edward made good on his promise to provide Radelmüller with passage back to Nova Scotia, and before the end of 1801 Radelmüller was back in Halifax. However, the government job he'd been offered the previous year had gone to someone else. The land he wanted was still available, though, but Radelmüller was obliged to become a steward in the household of Sir John Wentworth for two years.

"I found His Excellency a very just and good Governor," Radelmüller wrote. But John Paul was approaching forty, old age in those times, and he wanted something of his own. He wrote that he wished to "redire [*sic*] a little before I die in my own way." He learned that farmland in Upper Canada was better than in Nova Scotia. He gave Wentworth six months notice and made plans to head west.

Wentworth promised to provide Radelmüller with letters of recommendation and character — essential to a man (especially a foreigner) going to a place where he would be a stranger with no connections. Despite his promises, Wentworth was reluctant to let go of a quality servant like Radelmüller. On November 23, 1803, with his belongings on a ship and an impatient captain waiting for him to get aboard, Radelmüller was dismayed to learn that Wentworth did not have his papers ready. This, Radelmüller wrote, "hurted my feelings very much."

Wentworth wanted Radelmüller to stay with him for another year, but the German had his mind made up. The governor reluctantly agreed to send the papers to Upper Canada by mail. Radelmüller wrote, "I took the Resolution to set off in the name of God and a fair Wind for Upper Canada without the least Recommendations or Character, except a Clear Conscience and a Burs [purse] full of money, and I am in Expectation to get better used."

Radelmüller reached York, Upper Canada, on January 1, 1804. His papers from Wentworth would not arrive for another seven months. It appears to have taken some coaxing from Peter Hunter, the Lieutenant Governor of Upper Canada, to persuade Wentworth to send them.

After living in royal households in England and the governor's mansion in Halifax, Radelmüller must have found Little York something of a shock. It was a tiny, muddy, rough-hewn frontier community perched on the north shore of Lake Ontario. Beyond the little town lay a howling wilderness in which settlers struggled to clear land for farms. Natives came to trade their furs, and soldiers drilled in the rough fort just to the west of the town. For off-duty soldiers and farmers looking for a break from their labours, the only diversion was drinking.

However, Radelmüller was not a man to spend his time "in idleness," as he put it. He established a school in Markham Township where he taught English to German settlers. These were the "Pennsylvania Dutch" who had come to Upper Canada after the American Revolution. In 1804 Radelmüller was recognized by the colonial government as the official interpreter for these settlers in all their legal dealings.

More than anything else, Radelmüller wanted land. The best land in and around York and Markham had already been taken, except for numerous tracts that had been set aside as Crown Reserve. Radelmüller asked, humbly and as a man who "fears God and honors the King," if one of those Crown tracts could be made available for him. It was in support of this request that Radelmüller began writing the letters outlining his life of service to the royal family, perhaps hoping that this connection would work in his favour. Unfortunately, it didn't. Governor Hunter said no: Crown Reserve land was untouchable. Four years later Radelmüller submitted the same request to the new Lieutenant Governor, Major Francis Gore. Again he was turned down.

Then on July 24, 1809, Gore made Radelmüller the first keeper of the new lighthouse on Gibraltar Point. This stone tower was the first permanent lighthouse erected anywhere on the Great Lakes, and the position of lightkeeper was a plum job for a man like Radelmüller. It paid better than teaching English, and he was provided with a one-and-a-half storey cabin of logs and clapboard beside the tower.

Keeping the lighthouse was a position of considerable responsibility, because water was still the principal means of transportation in the Great Lakes region. Radelmüller not only had to keep the whale oil lamp burning at night and during foul weather, but also use signal flags to inform the harbour master of the approach of incoming traffic. That Radelmüller was chosen for the job indicates that the lieutenant governor considered him a responsible and reliable man.

At that time Toronto Island was still a peninsula that curved around the Bay of Toronto like a protective arm. Eventually storms would wash away the narrow spit connecting it to the mainland. It was still a wild, forested place, barred from settlement because it was all Crown Reserve. The most frequent visitors were duck hunters and fishermen who were usually gone by sundown. The lighthouse would have been a lonely place at night.

But the new lightkeeper did not remain lonely for long. On March 20, 1810, Radelmüller married Magdalena Burkholder in St. James Cathedral. She was from a Pennsylvania Dutch family and was much younger than John Paul. The couple had a daughter, Arabella, who was born before the end of 1810.

The main source we have for information on John Paul Radelmüller's life are the letters he wrote to governors in Upper Canada to support his requests for Crown Reserve land. After he was given the lightkeeping job, he recorded nothing more. We can only speculate on the last few years of his life and his untimely death.

Radelmüller was the Gibraltar Point lightkeeper during tumultuous times. War with the United States broke out in 1812. On April 27, 1813, the Americans came across Lake Ontario to attack York. After a sharp fight, the outnumbered British garrison retreated. But they blew up their powder magazine, inflicting many casualties on the enemy. One of the American dead was the noted explorer, General Zebulon Pike. The infuriated invaders looted York before putting it to the torch. But they gave the lighthouse a wide berth, fearing it had been mined. The Gibraltar Point lighthouse was the only structure that was not destroyed or damaged during the American occupation.

By a twist of fate it wasn't the American soldiers who were responsible for John Paul Radelmüller's death, but — if the sketchy evidence is accurate — British soldiers! There are several versions of what happened to Radelmüller out on Gibraltar Point.

The basic scenario they all share is that on the night of January 2, 1815, two or three soldiers from the York garrison went out to the lighthouse to get beer. Apparently Radelmüller brewed his own German-style beer and sold some of it to make a little extra money. One tale has it that he was a smuggler who brought in contraband booze from the United States, watered it down, and sold it at inflated prices. While cross-border smuggling was indeed rampant during the war, it would seem to have been quite out of character for Radelmüller to have engaged in such activities. Moreover, if he were caught smuggling, it could have cost him his position as lightkeeper.

In one account of the murder, the soldiers were already drunk when they arrived at the lighthouse, and became violently angry when Radelmüller refused to sell them beer. In another version, he sat down to have a few pints with the soldiers, but then cut them off when they became quarrelsome. In yet another tale, the drunken soldiers angrily accused Radelmüller of overcharging them.

The besotted soldiers allegedly fell upon the fifty-two-year-old lightkeeper and beat him to death. Again, the accounts differ. One story says the soldiers battered Radelmüller with a piece of firewood. Another says they used their belts on him, pounding him with the heavy buckles. In a third tale, Radelmüller sought refuge in the lighthouse. The soldiers broke down the door and pursued him to the top. They beat him senseless, then threw him over the side to his death. In all of these stories the soldiers, fearful of the consequences should their crime be discovered,

Art Gallery of Ontario

The Gibraltar Point Lighthose in 1820. In 1815 the first light keeper, John Paul Radelmüller, mysteriously disappeared, allegedly a murder victim.

dismembered Radelmüller's body and buried the parts at different locations on the peninsula.

There are several problems with these rather melodramatic accounts. Where were Magdalena and Arabella? Would intoxicated soldiers have been capable of carving up a body and scattering the parts in secret burial places? Considering it was January, the ground was probably frozen solid: would these secret burial places have been at all possible?

The fact remains that John Paul Radelmüller disappeared overnight. There is no surviving record of just how the people of York became aware of the murder, but on January 14, 1815, the *York Gazette* reported:

> Died on the evening of the 2nd of January, J.P. Radan Muller, keeper of the lighthouse on Gibraltar Point. From circumstances there is moral proof of his having been murdered. If the horrid crime admits of aggravation when the inoffensive

and benevolent character of the unfortunate sufferer are considered, his murder will be pronounced most barbarous and inhuman. The parties lost with him are the proposed perpetrators and are in prison.

This scanty report raises questions. What were the "circumstances"? What is meant by "the parties lost with him"? Could it mean that Radelmüller and the soldiers were first reported as missing; that after the murder the soldiers had tried to run? Could that be the reason that twelve days passed before news of the murder appeared in the *Gazette*? Were Radelmüller's remains actually found?

Two soldiers, John Henry and John Blowman, were arrested. No record of their trial has come to light. There evidently was a trial, though, because the *Gazette* reported on April 15, 1815: "No conviction of the supposed murderers of J.P. Radan Muller." No one else was ever brought to trial for the murder and John Paul Radelmüller's story was eventually lost in the vagaries of legend.

A document dated December 13, 1816, shows that Magdalena Radelmüller received a patent for 200 acres of land, to be held in trust with her brother, Michael Burkholder. Radelmüller had never been able to realize his dream of owning land in Upper Canada, but the dream came true for his widow. Radelmüller's bloodline carried on through his daughter Arabella, who married a man named Adam Rupert and had seven children before her death in 1844.

In 1893 some human skeletal remains were found in a shallow grave not far from the lighthouse, but whether they were Radelmüller's could never be determined. They have long since disappeared. According to Toronto lore the Gibraltar Point lighthouse, now a historic site, is still haunted by the ghost of John Paul Radelmüller, servant to royalty and victim in one of Canada's oldest murder mysteries.

# 2.

# CATHERINE SNOW:
## *PETIT TREASON*

The island of Newfoundland was Britain's oldest colony. The Newfoundlanders rejected Canadian Confederation in 1867. Except for a twenty-seven-year period in the twentieth century when it held Dominion status, Newfoundland remained a British colony until its citizens finally voted in favour of Confederation; it became Canada's tenth province in 1949. When the new province of Newfoundland and Labrador officially became Canadian, such colourful and dramatic stories as the tragedy of Catherine Snow became part of the Canadian mosaic.

In the summer of 1833, John Snow was a prosperous farmer and fisherman in the little port of Salmon Cove in Port de Grave on the Conception Bay side of the Bay De Verde Peninsula, about seventy-five miles from St. John's. He and his wife Catherine had seven children, of whom the oldest was about seventeen years old. Snow was not a wealthy man, but he was well enough off that he could employ a servant named Catherine White to help his wife with the household chores. He also had a bonded man, twenty-eight-year-old Arthur Spring, who had been work-ing for him for two years. Spring's best friend was twenty-four-year-old Tobias Mandeville, a cooper in the nearby community of Bareneed and Catherine Snow's cousin. Because John Snow was illiterate, Mandeville would go to his house every Saturday to help him with his accounting. Spring, and many other people in the village, knew something that John Snow did not: Mandeville was having an affair with Catherine Snow, a woman who was considerably older than he, and who, according to one observer, had "a forbidding cast of countenance." Then, on the night of August 31, 1833, John Snow disappeared.

On that fateful afternoon, John and his wife went by boat to Bareneed to deliver some fish to a merchant. Later Snow went out alone to pick Mandeville up for his weekly accounting meeting. After her husband left, Catherine sent her two oldest daughters, Bridget and Eliza, along with Catherine White to nearby Cupids to attend a wake. Exactly what happened after that became a matter of considerable dispute.

A couple of days passed, and neighbours began to wonder what had become of Snow. In a small community, in which everybody knew everyone else's comings and goings, it was very unusual for a person to go missing. Catherine appeared unconcerned, but rumours began circulating that Snow had been murdered or had "made away with himself" (committed suicide). John Jacob, a merchant in Bareneed and the community's Conservator of the Peace, went to Robert John Pinsent, the Magistrate for Port de Grave, and reported Snow's disappearance.

Pinsent sent Constable John Bows to make some enquiries. The information the officer brought back was sufficient to convince Pinsent

The town and harbour of St. John's, Newfoundland, in the summer of 1831, two years before John Snow disappeared.

to look into things personally. He was particularly curious about Mrs. Snow's remark, as reported by Constable Bows, that she did not want the police to trouble themselves about her affairs. On September 3, Pinsent, Bows, and three or four other men went to the Snows's house. As they approached the fishing stage, Arthur Spring greeted them and directed their attention to the flake (a platform for drying fish) nearest to the stage. It was a mess: fish were strewn everywhere, and toplines and rinds (pieces of bark used to cover piled of fish) were in disarray. Spring said that everything had been in good order on the night of August 31, but he had found things in that disturbed state the following morning. He said that he believed robbers were responsible.

Pinsent and the others went into the house and found Catherine Snow sitting in the parlour with a few neighbours. He told her that they had come to make enquiries about her husband's mysterious disappearance, and he wanted her to tell him everything she knew about it; her statements would be taken down in writing.

Catherine told Pinsent about the trip she and John had made to Bareneed with the load of fish, and his return trip to fetch Tobias Mandeville. The two men arrived back about half an hour after sunset, she said. They moored the boat, locked the stage, and came up to the house and had supper.

Then, Catherine continued, John suddenly asked where Bridget and Eliza were. When she told him they had gone to the wake, he "got into a passion," as Catherine put it, and threatened dire consequences if the girls did not return home soon. Mandeville and Spring left for the wake, leaving only John, Catherine, and their younger children in the house.

Catherine said that after supper John lay down for a rest, but he was still angry at her for letting their daughters go to the wake. After a few minutes he got up and took down a loaded gun that he kept on a rack. He went outside and fired it. Then he came back in, replaced the gun on the rack, and lay down again. He did not say why he had fired the gun, and she didn't ask him. People would later testify to having heard a gunshot that night.

After a little while, John told her that he was going to the wake to bring his daughters home. Catherine told Pinsent that she had been afraid, and tried to reassure John that the girls would come home with Mandeville and Spring, so John changed his mind about going out, and lay down again. Then, at about midnight, he got up. He put on his hat and his best blue waistcoat, but not his jacket. He left the house without saying a word.

Catherine explained to Pinsent that because of her husband's moody, angry behaviour, she was afraid to stay in the house. She put all but her youngest child to bed, and then took the little one with her to John's brother Edward's house. As she entered the house, which was only 100 yards from hers, she heard John shooing some pigs away from the door and knew he was home. Her brother-in-law was away, but his wife Ruth took Catherine in and listened to her talk about the troubles at home. Catherine asked a woman who was visiting Ruth to return home with her, but the woman declined, so Catherine stayed the night with her sister-in-law.

At approximately three o'clock in the morning, Bridget and Eliza arrived at Edward Snow's house. They had returned from the wake, and were surprised to find the house in darkness. Ruth asked them if their father had chastised them for being at the wake so late, but the girls said they had not seen him.

The following morning, Catherine said that she returned home expecting to find John, and was alarmed when he wasn't there. She knew he'd been home, because his hat and blue waistcoat were there. She searched all over the property, including the stage. Then she had Spring, Mandeville, and some neighbours help her search the community. There was no sign of John. Still, Catherine said she did not think he had met with any sort of foul play.

Pinsent didn't find Catherine's story very credible. He'd heard about the relationship between her and Mandeville, and a local man had speculated that John Snow had "gone off in a fit of jealousy." Pinsent questioned Spring and Mandeville, but they claimed to know nothing about Snow's disappearance. Pinsent wasn't convinced. On September 5 he had them arrested on suspicion of murder.

Both men immediately requested bail. A potential bondsman was prepared to post bail for Mandeville, but he withdrew when he heard a rumour that Mandeville was planning to flee. Catherine Snow became quite annoyed when she learned of the arrest. Catherine allegedly sent a friend to advise Spring to speak only in Gaelic when he was questioned. She told Pinsent that she needed Spring to harvest her hay and potatoes or she would lose both crops, but he advised her to hire someone else.

At first, Spring and Mandeville were kept under guard in separate locations. But Pinsent realized that if he put them together, they might give something away in their conversation. He confined them to adjoining cells in the Port de Grave "lock-up house," which was also the magistrate's office. Unbeknownst to the prisoners, a man was hiding under the magistrate's desk.

Since they thought they were alone, Mandeville and Spring started talking about what had happened on the night of August 31. But Spring quickly realized there was someone else in the room, and cried out, "That man has been listening under the table!" As the eavesdropper fled from the room, Spring called after him, "What did you hear? What did you hear?"

Soon after, Spring sent word to Pinsent that he had something important to tell him. On Pinsent's orders, Spring was manacled and brought before him. The prisoner's first words to Pinsent were, "We killed him; Mandeville and myself, and Mrs. Snow."

In a confession, that Pinsent said was given freely and without coercion, Spring told a story that was very different from Catherine's. He said they had been planning Snow's murder for about a month. He claimed that it was Mandeville's idea to kill Snow. He said that Mandeville had said that if they killed Snow, "We would have good times of it afterwards."

Spring said that he had told Mandeville that Snow often mistreated him, and it was then that Mandeville said they should kill Snow. Spring said that he didn't want to kill his master, just give him a good beating. But Mandeville said the best plan was to "murder Snow outright, and get him out of the place altogether."

About a week later, Catherine Snow told him that she wanted her husband dead. She claimed that Snow beat her, and that if he was not "put out of the way," he would eventually kill her or someone else in the family. When he heard that, Spring became part of the murder plot.

At first the conspirators planned to kill Snow with a hatchet while he worked in the stage. That idea came to naught when Spring's nerve failed him. After that, Catherine took charge.

As we already know, on the evening of August 31, after Snow had left for Bareneed to get Mandeville, Catherine sent Eliza and Bridget to the wake with her servant. Then, according to Spring, she called him to the house and told him that if he and Mandeville really intended to kill her husband, now was the time. She gave him some rum, then handed him Snow's gun. She told him to wait at the stage, and kill Snow when he returned with Mandeville.

Fortified by liquor, Spring went to the stage and waited inside. Half an hour later, at about ten o'clock, Snow and Mandeville arrived. While Snow moored the boat, Mandeville got out and went into the stage.

Mandeville saw the gun in Spring's hands and immediately knew what was up. He told Spring to shoot Snow as soon as he stepped onto the wharf. But Spring wasn't the one who shot Snow — or so he told Pinsent. He said his hands were trembling so badly that he dropped the gun.

"What are you about?" Mandeville had whispered. Spring said he couldn't do it. Mandeville told him to get out of the way, and picked up the gun. John Snow was just entering the stage when Mandeville shot him in the chest from about ten feet. He fell dead without so much as a groan.

Spring and Mandeville tied a grapnel (a small anchor) to the body, rowed it out to deep water, and sank it. Then they returned to the house and told Catherine what they had done. She told them to say nothing about it, and went to Edward Snow's house. The murderers went to the wake. The following morning, on Catherine's orders, they tossed around some of the fish and rinds on Snow's flake to make it seem as though thieves had been there.

Spring told Pinsent that Catherine and Mandeville planned to get married. They'd intended to sell Snow's property and move away. He said that Mandeville had promised him he that would be paid the full wages owed to him by Snow, and he would then be free to "quit the country."

News of Spring's confession spread rapidly. When Mandeville heard about it, he fainted in his cell. Constable Bows and some men were dispatched to arrest Catherine Snow, but when they arrived at her house, she had fled, leaving her children behind. A few days later she was found hiding in a neighbour's house.

A search of John Snow's stage turned up fresh bloodstains that someone had evidently tried to remove. Men in boats dragged the area where Spring said Snow's body had been dumped, but found nothing. There were sharks in the area, and they might have devoured it.

On September 8, Spring and Mandeville were handcuffed together and placed in a boat for the trip to Portugal Cove, where they would be transferred to a stagecoach and taken to St. John's. During the crossing, Mandeville said to the escorting officers, "I declare to you, as it were in the presence of God, and as a man who has no hope of life, and no inducement to tell an untruth, that I did not fire the gun, but this man [Spring] fired the gun."

Immediately, Spring shouted, "No! No! I did not! It was you who fired the gun."

"How can you tell such a lie?" Mandeville replied. "You know it is false!"

Mandeville admitted to being present when Spring shot Snow, and he confessed that he had been involved in an illicit affair with Mrs. Snow. He asked the officers if there was any chance for him. They told him they did not know, and advised him to admit to nothing.

The charge against Mandeville was a straightforward one of murder. However, under English law, Catherine and Spring were charged with *petit treason*. This referred to the murder of a husband by his wife, or a master by his servant. The punishment was the same: death by hanging. But *petit treason* was considered a particularly heinous crime against the established order, and the chances of the death sentence being commuted were much less. Wives simply could not be allowed to get away with killing their husbands, nor servants their masters.

Catherine changed her story. She said that on the night of August 31, Spring took Snow's gun to shoot some dogs. This was not unusual, because dogs sometimes got at the fish drying on the flakes. She said she told Spring not to hurt himself, to which he replied, "Never mind, I'm not going to hurt myself with it."

He went out, she said, and about three-quarters of an hour later she heard a shot. Then Spring and Mandeville came into the house. When she asked, "Where is the master?" Spring replied that he would soon be in. After a while, Catherine wondered aloud what could be keeping John, when his supper was ready. Mandeville said, "Cheer up your heart. There is nothing the matter." Catherine said the two men then left to pay their respects at the wake, and she went to Edward Snow's house.

She said she knew nothing about her husband's death except that Spring had confessed to murdering him. Catherine also claimed that after Magistrate Pinsent's initial visit to her house, Spring threatened to kill her if she had said anything about quarrels he'd had with Snow.

The trial of Catherine Snow, Tobias Mandeville, and Arthur Spring began on January 10, 1834, before Chief Justice Henry John Boulton. The case had generated a great deal of interest throughout Newfoundland, and the St. John's courtroom was packed. Prosecuting for the Crown was James Simms, the Attorney General of Newfoundland. Two St. John's lawyers defended the accused: George H. Emerson for Mandeville and Mrs. Snow, and Bryan Robinson for Spring.

In his opening address Prosecutor Simms stated that the crime of which the defendants stood accused was, "in its character the most deeply atrocious and appalling that I have ever seen." He outlined how the trio had plotted the murder and then carried it out.

"Mandeville was to leave Snow securing the boat and Spring would shoot him as he stepped onto the wharf. The two would then get rid of the body in the open sea. I can't prove which one fired the gun, but they were both present for the murder. As to Catherine Snow, there is no direct or positive evidence of her guilt. But I have a chain of circumstantial evidence to show her guilt."

Simms spoke in detail of how Catherine was an accessory before and after the fact. She had conspired to murder her husband, and after the shooting she had obstructed the police investigation with false statements. The prosecutor took care to point out to the jury, "That an illicit criminal intercourse had, during several years past, subsisted between the prisoners Catherine Snow Mandeville; and that as John Snow's existence was incompatible with the free exercise of their lustful gratifications, they had for a long time past determined to murder him, and had solicited and found a willing and ready associate in the diabolical plot, in the person of Arthur Spring."

Moreover, Simms said that Catherine had kept Mandeville, her lover, in her home for two nights after the murder. Then, having learned that Spring had confessed, she attempted to flee, abandoning her children. Simms hammered on the idea of the sheer treachery of the crime: John Snow had been plotted against and murdered by *his own wife, his own servant*, and *his intimate acquaintance*! The possibility that John Snow *might* have been a brutal husband and a harsh master had no bearing on the case.

The defence for Spring and Mandeville was that in the absence of a body, the Crown could not prove that a murder had taken place, regardless of what either of the two men had said; Catherine's situation was different. It was a given that either Spring or Mandeville had shot Snow in the presence of the other, making both equally guilty, but there was no evidence that Catherine had witnessed the crime or knew anything about it until after Spring's confession. Spring even testified that he had lied when he implicated her in the murder. But Simms argued that strong circumstantial evidence tied Catherine to the crime. Nonetheless, Catherine had many sympathizers in Newfoundland who believed she was innocent.

When all of the testimonies had been heard, and Judge Boulton gave his instructions to the jury, he drew particular attention to Catherine's case. He said that the jury must either acquit her or find her guilty of being an accessory to murder. She could not be convicted of the lesser charge of manslaughter.

"You will observe that nothing said by any of the prisoners can be admitted to implicate her in the act," he said. "However, her affair of passion with her very much younger cousin was enough to condemn her."

The jury took only half an hour to reach a verdict of guilty for all three accused. Boulton asked the doomed prisoners if they had anything to say before sentence was passed. Mandeville and Spring requested that after they were dead, their bodies be turned over to friends for Christian burial. At that time, the bodies of executed criminals were routinely given to medical schools for dissection.

"It is not in my power to comply with your request," the judge replied. "The law gives me no discretion in the matter."

Spring and Mandeville were sentenced to be hanged, after which their bodies would be dissected and then gibbeted on Spectacle Hill in Port de Grave. Gibbeting meant that the body was hung in chains in a public place, as a warning to others.

George Emerson stunned the court when he said that Catherine Snow was pregnant! Boulton ordered that Catherine be examined by midwives. The women confirmed that she was indeed with child, and Boulton postponed her execution until after she had delivered her baby.

There was no such reprieve for Spring and Mandeville; Newfoundland in the 1830s had no drawn out process of appeal. On January 13, barely three days after the trial, the condemned men were taken from their cells to the gallows that had been erected outside the courthouse. A large crowd had gathered for the public execution. The death march was interrupted when a slipper fell off Mandeville's foot, and he stooped to put it back on. According to the local newspaper, the *Newfoundlander*, "They died bravely, and their execution was witnessed by thousands."

Catherine Snow then had to endure a bizarre incarceration, awaiting her child's birth and her own death. Many people who believed her innocent were critical of Judge Boulton's remarks to the jury. Boulton, however, was unmovable. He said that Catherine had been found guilty of *petit treason*, and therefore deserved the sentence of the court.

As the weeks passed, Catherine showed no signs of contrition, and she steadfastly maintained her innocence. She prayed and fasted in her prison cell, but never spoke of her children. She once asked her priest, "Oh, sir, is there no hope?"

He replied, "No, my good lady. It is my duty to entreat you to lay aside such thoughts. It is only in heaven that your hopes are to rest."

Catherine's child was born in early July. Soon after, she was taken to the courtroom and informed that her execution would take place on the morning of July 21. Once again, she denied her guilt.

Two days before her date with the hangman, Catherine stopped eating. "Oh, what is nourishment to me?" she said. "God calls upon me to suffer death. That I cannot avoid, but let me add as much as possible to my sufferings so that I may try to make that death worthwhile." The night before the execution she drank a small amount of wine.

At three o'clock on the morning of July 21, Catherine's priest said mass in her cell. At five o'clock she was dressed in burial garb. When she realized that she was wearing her grave clothes, Catherine screamed and fell to her knees weeping. Then, supported by the priest, she regained her composure.

The gallows was just outside a window of the old St. John's Courthouse and Gaol. Window sashes had been removed so she could step out onto the platform. Before the noose was placed around her neck, Catherine spoke to the people who had come to watch her hang. "I was a wretched woman, but as innocent of any participation in the crime of murder as an unborn child."

Henry Winton, a local editor who witnessed the execution, wrote, "She proceeded to the gallows with a firm step and with a demeanor which indicated a resignation to her fate. She was conducted to the platform, attended by priests, shortly before the hour of nine o'clock, and the usual preliminaries having been arranged, the unhappy woman, after a few brief struggles, passed into another world."

The Catholic clergy of St. John's did not believe that Catherine's guilt had been proven, so they allowed her body to be buried in the consecrated ground of a Catholic cemetery. Even though she was legally tried, convicted, and executed, to many Newfoundlanders, Catherine Snow is a legendary martyr to a harsh, unjust judicial system. Her story inspired the 2009 novel *Catherine Snow*, by Newfoundland author Nellie. P Stowbridge.

# 3.

# DR. WILLIAM HENRY KING:
## A GRADUAL AND PAINFUL DEATH

What could be more sinister than a doctor, bound by the Hippocratic Oath to do no harm and in whom the patient has placed the utmost trust, who commits murder under the guise of administering medication? There have, in fact, been a few murderous doctors in recorded history. Perhaps the most infamous homicidal physician was Dr. Thomas Neill Cream who, in the latter part of the nineteenth century, left a trail of victims in Canada, the United States, and England before he finally ended his murderous career on the gallows in London's Newgate Prison in 1892. But a generation before Dr. Cream dispatched his first victim, another man of medicine stunned the citizens of Canada West (now Ontario) by committing the ultimate act of betrayal.

William Henry King was born in 1835 to a fairly prosperous farming family in the township of Sophiasburg in Prince Edward County, in the eastern part of what was then called Upper Canada. When William was eleven years old his family moved to the township of Cramahe, near Brighton at the eastern end of Lake Ontario. As the eldest son, William had to help with the farm work, so his formal schooling was limited to two months of the year. At that time many of the school teachers in rural areas were barely competent, so the quality of education was poor. Not that farm children were expected to learn much more than the basics of reading, writing, and a little arithmetic. William King's school days practically came to an end when, while he was in his mid-teens, his father became an invalid, and the burden of running the farm fell on the boy's shoulders.

However, William King did not want to spend the rest of his life behind a plow: he dreamed of becoming a doctor. When he had actually been able to attend school, he'd shown himself to be a bright and eager student. On the farm, in addition to doing all of the back-breaking chores, he did an admirable job of educating himself.

When William turned seventeen in 1851, he persuaded his father to send him to the Normal School (teacher's college) in Toronto during the winter months, when he could be spared from chores on the farm. He lived frugally and studied hard. In 1855 King passed his final exams with flying colours. He was given a first class teaching certificate, and landed a good position at the Central School of Hamilton, teaching physiology. King would later say that he was now "in a fair way to achieve both fame and wealth."

Young King had a lot of things going for him. He was intelligent, and at twenty he had already received a better education than most farm boys could ever hope for. He was good-looking, stood five-foot-seven, had dark eyes, a pale but clear complexion, dark hair, and a fashionably trimmed moustache and beard. His principal vanity seems to have been a desire to give people the impression that he was "deeply learned."

King lived by a strict Christian moral code. He abstained from alcohol and never set foot in a brothel. He attended church on Sunday without fail. According to his own account, "I never went to the theatre but once in my life; and the thought to swear did not come into my mind from one year's end to another."

While King was teaching in Hamilton, he met Dr. Greenlees, who encouraged him to study medicine. This advice would send King to a medical college in Philadelphia. Meanwhile, the young man had become smitten with a local girl.

Sarah Anne Lawson came from a large, well-off, and very respectable family who owned a farm about a mile from Brighton. Sarah, who was about King's age, was very attractive and well-educated. She and King were married in 1855. They moved into a house in Hamilton, and took in boarders to help pay the bills. Sarah's father, John, also assisted the young couple financially. John Lawson must have seen a bright future for his new son-in-law, because he even agreed to help pay for King's medical studies in the U.S.

Unfortunately, marital bliss was short-lived. Sarah gave birth to a baby girl who was physically handicapped. The child lived for only a month. Sarah complained that her husband showed no affection for the baby; she suspected him of being responsible for the infant's death. Sarah moved back to her parents' home, partly because of poor health, but also because she said that King had been abusive toward her.

In turn, King accused his wife of infidelity. King wrote an angry letter to John Lawson, giving details of her alleged unfaithfulness. Later, he apologized for the letter. His father-in-law returned it to him, but only after making a copy.

From 1856 to 1858, King was in Canada only during the summer months, teaching at various schools near Brighton. The rest of the time he was in Philadelphia pursuing his medical studies. He was a top student. In 1857, King was elected president of the Hahnemannian Medical Institute of the Homeopathic Medical College of Philadelphia. He graduated near the top of his class in 1858, and went home with diplomas from the Homeopathic Medical College, the Pennsylvania Medical University in Philadelphia, and the Eclectic Medical College of Philadelphia.

On King's return in March 1858, he and Sarah reconciled. They moved into a house in Brighton, and Dr. King began to build up a very successful practice. His patients considered him a "pleasant and gentlemanly" doctor, with manners that were "easy and graceful." Before long he was earning $100 to $200 a month, which was a very comfortable income for a small-town doctor at that time. But even though husband and wife appeared to have patched up their differences, all was not well in the King household.

Dr. King's wandering eye had fallen on an attractive young lady named Dorcas Garret, who lived with her father on a farm in Murray Township, near Brighton. King wrote Dorcas a letter in which he said he was in love with her. His wife, he said, was ill and would soon die, and he wanted Dorcas to be the new Mrs. King. Dorcas's reply was a sharp refusal. She also threatened to expose King if he made any further advances on her. Sarah knew nothing about any of this.

On September 23, 1858, a friend of the Lawson family, Miss Melinda Vandervoort, visited the King home. Melinda, who lived in Sidney Township near Trenton, was twenty years old, very pretty, and had been spending a few days with Sarah's parents. Dr. King had never met her before. That evening, after King and Sarah had driven Melinda back to the Lawson farm, Sarah told her husband about a peculiar thing Melinda had said to her.

Sarah said that Miss Vandervoort had told her she was in love with Dr. King. She had been in love with him from the moment she'd seen his photograph in the Lawson home. Sarah apparently did not respond to Melinda's very forward statement. When Dr. King heard of it, he seemed to just brush it aside as nonsense.

But the idea of a beautiful young woman falling in love with his photograph appealed to Dr. King's vanity. Melinda visited again the next day and, at Dr. King's request, stayed until late in the evening. Like many Victorian middle-class families, the Kings had a piano and a melodeon in the parlour. Melinda could play both instruments, and also had a lovely singing voice. She entertained Dr. and Mrs. King with renditions of popular songs, such as "Kitty Clyde," "Old Dog Gray," and "Hazel Dell." Dr. King was soon infatuated with Melinda. Sarah, who could neither play a note nor sing, seemed rather drab in comparison. What's more, Sarah was now about three months pregnant.

After she returned to her home in Sidney Township, Melinda sent King a daguerreotype of herself. He quickly wrote her a letter in response. (In Victorian love letters it is not unusual to see words like *love* and *heart* represented only by the first letter.)

Sweet little lump of good nature.

I long looked with prudent anxiety for the arrival of the object of my thoughts but began to despair. Still, I had too much perseverance to give up, and alas, I walked to the P.O. this morning (Monday) and found the most precious thing (except the original) on earth. Better than all California. I will not, however, tell you what it was, but could I indulge in the hope that those winning and genial smiles would ever be found in my possession, all troubles would then cease. It is a perfect infatuation to me. Can you keep from sacrificing yourself on the hymeneal altar for the next year? I wish so. Now I am at a loss to know whether to take this as a token of friendship or l___. Will you inform me which you mean it for, and if the latter it will certainly soothe and refresh my drooping spirits? All you say shall be perfectly confidential. You need never have the least suspicion of this token being seen or handled by any other than its present possessor. Furthermore, if you correspond with me I will guarantee upon my word and honour that detection shall never happen. You are therefore perfectly safe, but oh I could but know whether you could reciprocate my feelings or not. Much would I give to be assured on this point. It might give me the most exquisite joy, or might cause me bitter pain. Yet this token shall cheer me many a time while riding through the long mile.

I must claim your indulgence that your sense of propriety and good taste will pardon me for thus punctually giving expression to my feelings. Do not betray the confidence I have reposed in you. O l___ I would like to say a thousand things to you that flash through my imagination like panoramic display, but I must not venture for the present. May I hear from the object so dear to my h____? Why is it so, you might ask? Well, I would like to tell that some other time.

Please accept ten thousand thanks for such a treasure as I received this morning. It shall always remain in my possession unless called for by its identity. O l___ lovely smiles so plainly denigrated, I must think you meant for something. I cannot possibly be deceptious. I have told you enough that you may judge pretty nearly where my h____ is, now could you be induced to tell me where your's (sic) is? O do!

You will observe that this letter is anonymous for fear somebody might get your keys and read it. As it is if they should, they would not be the wiser, but my name shall be ___. You know whom it is from just as well as if my name was appended. Do you remember ___ and cc, cc and 'going to California', well when you write, sign *Van*. Do not judge of my literary attainments from the style of these hastily thrown together sentences, for I paid more attention to ideas than style. Come and visit us whenever you can. _____ is very sick. Last night we thought she would die.

Your sincere l___

The sick person referred to in the last line was obviously Sarah, who was actually in perfect health. She would not remain so for long. Meanwhile, Melinda wrote back to King:

Dear Doctor.

The time has come for me to respond. Yours of the 10th instant came to hand in good repair, and exceedingly pleased was I while perusing its contents. It is with much pleasure, but at the same time a degree of embarrassment that I embrace the opportunity to write you one. I feel an unusual warmth of friendship for you, and not being in the habit of portraying my weakness by way of the pen, expect to find it no easy task — however, hope it will be accepted. I hardly know in what manner to address you, as circumstances are with you, it appears almost in vain for me to think of you only as a friend. Yet something seems to whisper "still hope."

Since I first had the pleasure of an introduction, my heart is constantly with you, and I'm not contented a moment. O l____ could I forever be with you, I think I could be happy, for indeed I enjoyed myself to excess during my stay in your presence, though suppose now I must eradicate such thoughts from my mind; for you are married, and my destiny must be to *love* you and not share your interesting society. We are some distance apart, yet trust our ties of friendship, although of short production, are such as not to allow time or distance to sever. Perhaps you'll pardon my familiarity when you come to realize that you have unlinked the tender cord of affection until you have an alarming influence over my girlish nature.

One smile only from your countenance can inspire a depth of veneration in my bosom never felt by me for any individual. Well now, Dr, don't you consider it very wrong for me to correspond with you. I'm afraid if known it would destroy "Annie's" happiness, and for instance if I was in her position, I *would* much rather be in my *grave* than suffer the idea of your intimacy with another, though perhaps you merely express some of your ideas to me for pastime so I hope you'll not [illegible] them, for I am easily flattered, and it may prove to be serious. I am very lonely … Please answer, if you deem me worthy. I hope you'll not criticize.

Your unwavering
Van

The idea of sending Sarah to her grave had already occurred to Dr. King. On October 14, four days before Melinda wrote her letter, Sarah suddenly became very ill. She suffered from excruciating abdominal cramps, accompanied by violent bouts of vomiting and diarrhea. Of course, her husband was her physician. He told Sarah that she had *cholera morbus*, which was the nineteenth century term for what is now called acute gastroenteritis. He also said she had an ulcerated womb.

King prescribed medication for Sarah, administering it himself. Sarah's condition worsened. During the weeks of Sarah's illness, Dr. King frequently prayed aloud for her recovery, but told her family, and

Sarah herself, that as a doctor he had little hope. Still, he insisted that she take the medicine he prescribed, a whitish powder mixed with water. Sarah complained that it had a "fiery" taste. Sometimes she would vomit immediately after swallowing it. Then she would beg her husband not to make her take anymore. King would prepare another dose and tell her to try hard to keep it down, gently arguing that the medicine was her only chance for survival.

At John Lawson's angry insistence, another physician, Dr. A. E. Fife, was called to Sarah's sick room. He examined her and prescribed a different medication. Miraculously, Sarah began to improve.

Her husband, mother, and father had been taking turns sitting up with her through the long nights, but on the evening of November 3, 1858, Sarah told them she felt well enough that they could all go to bed and get a good night's sleep. The following morning they found Sarah, in bed: she had sunk into a coma. By nightfall she was dead.

King put on a dramatic display of grief. So extreme were his lamentations, that another doctor had to be called to the house. King was given a sedative, and fell into a deep sleep. He awoke the next day, composed enough to make the necessary arrangements.

At Sarah's funeral Dr. King was once again overwhelmed with grief. There wasn't a soul present who didn't feel sympathy for the bereaved young doctor — except the family of the deceased!

The Lawsons were very suspicious about Sarah's death. John Lawson wondered why King had been so set against having another doctor examine Sarah when his own treatment clearly was not working. John and his wife, Elizabeth, had been in the house for most of Sarah's illness, and had seen King administering the medication. Elizabeth had changed the soiled bed sheets after Sarah vomited. They had heard her plead with him not to be given any more, and had heard King insisting she take it if she hoped to recover. At the time the Lawsons did not realize that William King was slowly murdering their daughter. After all, he was a doctor.

But the Lawsons couldn't accept that Sarah died so suddenly and so soon after showing such great improvement under Dr. Fife's care. Nor were they fooled by King's exaggerated displays of grief, which enhanced their suspicions that King had poisoned Sarah.

At some point, either during Sarah's illness or during the funeral, Elizabeth searched King's coat pockets. She found the picture of Melinda Vandervoort, as well as her letter. She didn't take them, nor did she tell King she had seen them. Instead she told him she had heard a rumour that he carried around a likeness of Miss Vandervoort. King denied having any such picture.

After Sarah's funeral, Elizabeth told people about the picture and letter. Soon the story was being spread from township to township. Dorcas Garrett heard it, and came forward with her own story of a letter from Dr. King. Then it was discovered that King had purchased considerable amounts of arsenic and morphine. Both drugs were commonly used by nineteenth century doctors, but there was sufficient circumstantial evidence of foul play for authorities to summon a coroner's jury and order the body to be exhumed. The liver and stomach were removed and sent to the University of Toronto for examination.

Dr. King was out of town visiting patients when the inquest was called. It was in session when he returned to Brighton. John Lawson took grim satisfaction in personally telling him about it. Pretending to be outraged, King declared he would put a stop to the inquest. He climbed into his carriage and drove off at great speed. But he did not go to the schoolhouse where the inquest was being held. Instead, he rushed off to Sidney Township.

It was late in the evening when King reached the Vandervoort farm. John and Elizabeth, Melinda's parents, had never met King before and his reason for coming alarmed them. King said that his wife's body was being exhumed and that soon a warrant for his arrest would be issued. He said there would also be a warrant for Melinda's arrest. He wanted to take her to the United States where they would be safe until the trouble was straightened out.

Melinda's parents were reluctant to allow her to go with King, but the fear of her being arrested prevailed. They said she could go with King on the sole condition that the pair go to Melinda's aunt's house in Cape Vincent, New York, a small community on the St. Lawrence River.

At the University of Toronto, Henry Croft, a professor of chemistry, found traces of arsenic in Sarah's liver and stomach. A warrant was issued for King's arrest, and Sarah's brother, Clinton Lawson, was sworn in as a special constable to serve it.

It didn't take Lawson long to trace King to Cape Vincent. There he learned that King was staying at a farm owned by a man named Bate, about six miles inland. Accompanied by a United States Marshal named Gordon, Lawson went to the farm.

Marshal Gordon entered the house while Lawson waited in the yard. About three minutes later, Lawson saw Dr. King jump out a window and make a break for the woods. When King saw Lawson chasing him, he

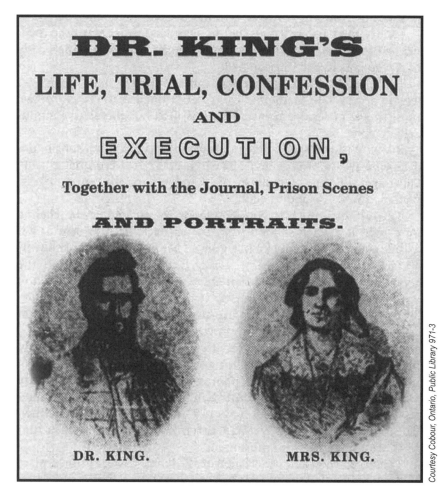

# DR. KING'S
# LIFE, TRIAL, CONFESSION
## AND
# EXECUTION,
### Together with the Journal, Prison Scenes
# AND PORTRAITS.

DR. KING.    MRS. KING.

The likenesses of Dr. William Henry King and his wife Sarah on the cover of an 1859 pamphlet about the murder.

turned and ran into the barn. Lawson followed, and found King hiding under some straw. He pulled a revolver and told King to come with him or be shot.

Clinton Lawson had no legal authority to seize King on American soil and drag him back to Canada, but U.S. Marshal Gordon must have looked the other way. Lawson ignored King's protests, and forced the doctor to accompany him to Cobourg where he was locked in jail. During King's trial a lawyer asked Lawson if the doctor had returned to Canada willingly. Lawson replied, "No, sir. No sir-ee!"

King's trial in the Cobourg courthouse began on April 4, 1859. The chief counsel for the defence was John H. Cameron, a lawyer said to have powerful political connections. Representing the Crown was Sir Thomas Galt, QC. Mr. Justice Burns presided. The case of the doctor accused of poisoning his own wife was a great sensation, and people came from miles around, by horse-drawn conveyance and by train, to watch the trial. The courtroom was filled to capacity, with many women learning, much to their collective dismay, that it was "no place to wear hoops." Those people who could not get in had to rely on accounts in newspapers like the *Toronto Globe*, which stated:

> The case is a remarkable one, both in a criminal and scientific point of view. If the prisoner be found guilty, another instance will be added to those already on record wherein a knowledge of medicine has been put to the worst possible purpose – wherein the physician has cruelly, persistently and remorselessly used his skill for the destruction of life under the pretence of saving, wherein the husband has stood by the bedside of his dying wife, and while speaking to her words of comfort, and of hope, has betrayed her to a gradual and painful death … this case bids fair to become famous in Canadian criminal records.

The first witness for the Crown, Professor Henry Croft, testified that he found arsenic in Sarah's stomach and liver. He said the amounts were small, but sufficient to cause death. Expert witnesses for the defence, including Dr. A.H. Flanders and Professor O.J. Hempel of Philadelphia, testified that the amounts of arsenic found in the organs were too small to have been fatal. They said it was hardly surprising that arsenic should be in Mrs. King's body, since it was used in many homeopathic remedies. Professor Croft, they pointed out, was a chemist, not a physician, and therefore was not wholly qualified to make statements on the use of arsenic in medications prescribed by doctors. In cross-examination, Croft said that he knew that a sixteenth of a grain of arsenic was the usual dose a patient was given. He had found eleven grains in Sarah's stomach.

One of the Americans then suggested that the arsenic could have been added after the stomach was removed from the body. This brought on a round of hissing from the spectators. Justice Burns put a quick stop to that.

The jury then heard from a succession of witnesses that included the local coroner, several doctors, a railway conductor, and an express agent. They described the stomach's journey in a corked pickle jar, from the time it was removed from the body in Brighton until it arrived at Professor Croft's laboratory in Toronto. At no point had there been an opportunity for anybody to tamper with the bottle's contents.

Other doctors testifying for the Crown supported Croft's opinion that Sarah had died from arsenic poisoning. The physicians speaking for the defence conceded that arsenic could have caused Sarah's death, but they added that it could very well have been unintentional. In his desire to cure his wife of her illness, they said, Dr. King could have given Sarah an amount of arsenic that would not have killed a healthy person, but which proved too much for Sarah in her weakened state.

John and Elizabeth Lawson's emotion-charged testimony, as they gave eyewitness accounts of Sarah's last days must have had a profound effect on each member of the jury. Descriptions of the doomed woman's pitiful pleas to be given no more of the medication, while her husband pressed it on her, must have been absolutely heart-rending to the people who heard them. It seemed possible that Dr. King had unintentionally poisoned his wife. But what about Melinda Vandervoort?

When Melinda was called to the stand, she admitted that she knew Dr. King, but that there had been no improper relations between them.

She claimed that she'd sent her picture to Dr. King, with the intention that he give it to Mrs. King. Melinda claimed that when she received what appeared to be a love letter from Dr. King, she found it funny, and that she had written her reply only "for amusement." Prosecutor Galt told Melinda to leave the courtroom while he read the letters aloud for the jury. As King listened from the prisoner's box, he smiled, as though he, too, found it all very amusing.

Throughout the two days of the trial, King was composed and seemed to be confident that he would be acquitted. Though opinion in the street seemed to be strongly against him, Cameron had brought in an impressive array of character witnesses: medical colleagues who testified that King was a fine doctor; professors from Philadelphia who described him as one of the best students in their college; patients who said they had received excellent care from Dr. King; and local civic authorities who said they had known William King for many years and did not believe him capable of murder. Moreover, while in jail, King had received letters from many prominent and respectable men in both Canada and the United States, offering him their moral support.

When all the evidence was in, Cameron and Galt each made impassioned addresses to the jury. Justice Burns carefully summarized the points the Crown and the defence had made. In his instructions to the jury, he stated that they must give the accused the benefit of any doubt they might have about his guilt.

The jury retired at three o'clock in the afternoon, and did not reach a verdict until ten o'clock the following morning. Dr. King was stunned when he heard it: Guilty! But with a strong recommendation for mercy.

Under British law, if a jury found a defendant guilty of a capital crime, the judge was obliged to pronounce the death sentence, despite any recommendation for mercy. It was then up to the government to consider whether or not the sentence should be commuted to life imprisonment. Justice Burns sentenced King to be hanged outside the county courthouse in Cobourg on June 9, 1859. Cameron made every effort to get a commutation, but the colonial administration did not share the jury's opinion that King should be shown mercy.

Not long before the appointed day, King confessed in writing that he had murdered Sarah. He said he'd done it because he believed that she had been unfaithful to him, and because he had become infatuated with Melinda Vandervoort. However, King said it was not arsenic that killed Sarah. King claimed that early in the morning of the day Sarah died, he had given her a drachm (the equivalent of an eighth of an ounce) of chloroform. He said she had begged him to release her, once and for all, from her pain and suffering. The doctor expressed bitter remorse for having committed the deed.

On the morning of June 9, some 5,000 spectators, many of them women and children, waited in front of the jail to watch William King hang. About a thousand of them had camped overnight to be assured a good view. A four-foot-high barricade in front of the courthouse kept the crowd back. Other than that, the execution would take place in full public view, as was the custom of the time. Newspapers reported that the crowd was very orderly.

Two days before the scheduled hanging, King's father came to visit him. They had a final parting that observers said was heart-breaking. No other member of the King family went to the jail, allegedly due to illness.

Curiously, King's last visitor, besides the clergymen who stayed with him through his final hours, was Clinton Lawson. The day before the execution, Lawson went to the jail and spoke to King for a long time. When they parted, they shook hands and asked each other's pardon.

Before King was taken from his cell to his appointment with the hangman, one of the clergymen gave him a picture of Sarah that he had gotten from Clinton. King clutched the picture in his hands, wept over it, and kissed it. He said he hoped to be with her soon.

At precisely eight o'clock, the sheriff led King outside and up the steps to the gallows. His face was wet with tears, but he ascended the ladder "with a firm step." In the shadow of the noose, King faced the multitude that had come to watch him die, and read a long, prepared statement. He said he had been a sinner and that he accepted his fate. Several times King expressed his belief that God had forgiven him. He urged his listeners to lead devout, Christian lives. He did not say a word about Sarah.

When King was finished, the executioner told him to kneel on the trap door. The hooded hangman tied King's hands and legs, pulled a white cloth cap over his head, and put the rope around his neck. At the sheriff's signal, the trap was sprung and King dropped. The fall did not break his neck, so he strangled. Half an hour later, the homicidal doctor was pronounced dead. No one in the silent crowd wept.

# 4.

# THE HARVEY MURDERS:
## OUT OF LOVE

On the evening of March 26, 1889, William H. Harvey of Guelph, Ontario, paced anxiously outside the Ellis Jewellery Store at the corner of King and Yonge Streets in Toronto. A short while earlier he had sent a note, by a messenger, to his seventeen-year-old son Willie, who was working in the city as an engraver's apprentice. Harvey had written:

> My Dear Boy.
>
> I am in town for the night. Will you come down and stay all night with me? Walk down the west side of Yonge Street and north side of King and Palmer House. I may come up to meet you.
>
> Your father.

The message, it was later noted, was written in a clear, steady hand.

With a cigar clenched in his teeth and his hands in his pockets, Harvey kept looking up Yonge Street, anticipating Willie's arrival. William Harvey had not travelled to Toronto for a fatherly visit with his son. He was there to kill Willie! He had a revolver in his pocket. Three of the gun's chambers had already been fired.

No one who knew William Harvey would have thought him capable of murder. He was a quiet, easy going man who from all appearances was dedicated to his wife, Matilda, and their children. His full beard made him look professorial, and he was quite well-educated. He was about fifty-five years of age, and stood just over six feet tall. Some people thought he looked "soldierly." He was very much involved with the activities of St. George's Anglican Church in Guelph; he was also the superintendent of its Sunday School. Harvey was said to have the manners of a gentleman, he did not drink, and he was well liked in the community. People often remarked about how he doted on his youngest child, little Geraldine. But few of Harvey's acquaintances in Guelph knew anything of his litany of past misfortunes.

The Harvey family had come to Canada from England in 1870, settling first in Montreal. Harvey invested whatever money he had in the publication of a new encyclopedia. The project failed and Harvey lost everything. Disaster struck when a diphtheria epidemic took three of his and Matilda's small children in a short period of time. Matilda later confided to a friend in Guelph about this tragedy, that the deaths of the children had changed William. He had forbidden her to ever speak of it in his presence.

In 1881, Harvey secured a job as an accountant with the Toronto Bolt Works Company, and moved his family to the city. Besides Willie and Geraldine, there was the eldest child, Lillian. Misfortune seemed to follow Harvey like a dark cloud. The Bolt Works Company went broke, leaving Harvey in dire financial straits once more. He was in debt, and the sheriff seized most of his household property.

Harvey managed to eke out a living doing temporary accounting work for various firms throughout the city. The family also made a little money on the side selling small wooden figures that Willie carved. But they barely managed to make ends meet, and Harvey's debts remained a burden. To make matters worse, Matilda and little Geraldine were often sick, adding medical bills to the household's costs.

Then Harvey's luck seemed to take a turn for the better. He found an accounting job with Toronto businessman E.R. Clarkson's firm. This new employer found that Harvey was a competent and hardworking bookkeeper. Eight months after Harvey started working for him, Clarkson learned that a friend and business associate in Guelph, James Walter Lyon, needed a good accountant to straighten out his books, which previous employees had left in disarray. Lyon was a wealthy and influential man in Guelph, and owned the World Publishing Company, as well as several other businesses.

Clarkson recommended William Harvey to Lyon, and Harvey went to Guelph to sort out Lyon's accounting problems. Harvey did such a good job that Lyon gave him a full-time, permanent position. Harvey moved his wife and daughters to Guelph, but Willie remained in Toronto where he was apprenticing as an engraver. The Harvey family took up residence in a modest stone house at the corner of Woolwich and Edwin streets, just a few minutes' walk from the downtown area. The family made friends, and things seemed to be going well for them at last. But Harvey still had those debts!

Lyon was very happy with Harvey's work. He told people Harvey was an excellent accountant and one of the best employees he'd ever had. Lyon paid Harvey the very reasonable wage of $25 a week, let him keep his own hours, and gave him a $50 bonus at Christmas.

Lyon was often out of town on business for extended periods of time, and would leave his office in the care of the trustworthy Harvey. When Lyon returned to Guelph it was usually for only short stays, during which he had no time to inspect the company books himself. At times there was as much as $16,000 in the company safe. Lyon had no reason to believe anything was amiss: he had complete confidence in Harvey, who was in charge of the money in Lyon's absence and had a key to the safe.

Then in March 1889, about eighteen months after Harvey had moved to Guelph, Lyon decided to take a four-week break from his business trips. It was about this time that Harvey's friends noticed that he'd become moody and withdrawn. Lyon had a lot of correspondence to catch up on, but he eventually got around to inspecting the books.

On Saturday, March 17, 1889, Lyon was surprised to see that nothing had been entered for four months. He told Harvey to get the records up to date immediately. It took repeated urgings, but by Thursday, March 21, Harvey had finished the job. On Friday evening Lyon closely examined the ledgers and found numerous inconsistencies for the period from April 1888 to February 1889. He estimated that about $700 was missing.

Lyon thought the matter over all weekend. On Monday morning he sent his other employees out of the office so he could confront Harvey privately. At first Harvey denied any wrongdoing. But with the evidence right there in black and white. He finally admitted that he had taken the money to pay debts.

William Harvey and his daughter Geraldine.

*Courtesy Guelph Public Library*

Just what was said between the two men is not known, but Harvey apparently came away from the meeting feeling that he and his employer could make some sort of arrangement and avoid involving the law. Lyon's wife, when she heard of the situation, pleaded with her husband not to press charges against the accountant. But Lyon had been the victim of embezzlement once before. Moreover, he felt that Harvey had not displayed much in the way of remorse; he had even argued that the amount taken was less than $1,000 — not much to a man of Mr. Lyon's means.

Lyon was also angered and hurt over the betrayal of trust. He decided to lay charges. Thus began a series of misjudgments that would, within a matter of hours, lead to something almost unheard of in Victorian Ontario: mass murder!

On the evening of Monday, March 25, 1889, Guelph Police Chief Frederick W. Randall arrested Harvey. Harvey's friend Dr. Stephen E. Lett, co-founder of the Guelph sanitarium called the Homewood Retreat (now the Homewood Health Centre), posted the $2,000 bail. Harvey was instructed to appear in court the following morning.

*Courtesy Guelph Police Services*

Guelph Police Chief Frederick Randall found the victims a short while after speaking to William Harvey.

Just after nine o'clock that Tuesday morning, Harvey went to Lyon's downtown office to confront him about why he'd changed his mind about laying charges. Lyon later recalled, "I said I hadn't changed my mind and I didn't think he was very penitent yet … I added, 'Mr. Harvey, I made you no promises what I should do.'" Harvey allegedly replied, "Certainly, I know you did not," and left without saying another word.

At about 9:30 a.m., Harvey walked into J.M. Bond's hardware store in downtown Guelph. After a little casual conversation with another customer, he told store clerk James Knowles he wanted to buy "a good revolver" that was to be charged to Mr. Lyon's account. He explained that an employee in Mr. Lyon's firm was going to Mexico and needed a weapon for protection.

Knowles knew both Harvey and Lyon well, and had no reason to be suspicious. He took Harvey to an upstairs room where the firearms were kept. Harvey chose a .32 calibre, silver plated, double-action Smith & Wesson five-shot revolver. He also took a box of fifty cartridges and went home. Two well-diggers were working in the backyard. Harvey gave them some money and sent them away.

Guelph was still a small town, and news travelled faster by word of mouth than by means of the press. Well before that day's edition of the *Guelph Mercury* carried the story of Harvey's arrest for embezzlement, the gossip mill had been working. Knowles heard the story only minutes after selling Harvey the gun. Fearing that Harvey intended to shoot Lyon, Knowles informed Chief Randall.

At about the same time, someone told Lyon that Harvey had just bought a gun. Alarmed, Lyon quickly dashed off a message to Randall. It said in part, "Mr. Harvey is a proud man and is evidently desperate. Whether he intends to use it [the gun] on me or himself I cannot tell, but in the meantime I want protection and you had better take the revolver from him."

Randall sent a constable named Kickley to Harvey's house. When Harvey came to the door, Kickley asked him about the gun. Harvey said he had bought the gun to protect himself, but that he and his employer had settled their problem amicably and he would be returning to his old position. He said he didn't want the humiliation of the police taking the gun away from him in his own home, as though he could not be trusted with it. He promised to return it to Bond's store himself within an hour. Harvey delivered this explanation in such a quiet, gentlemanly way, that Kickley was convinced there was no serious threat. He returned to the police station without the gun.

Not satisfied with Kickley's report, Chief Randall, accompanied by another policeman, started out for the Harvey home himself. On the way he met the rector of St. George's Church, Reverend George Harvey (no relation to William). Reverend Harvey had heard about William Harvey's arrest the night before, as well as the purchase of the gun that morning. As a close friend and spiritual advisor of the Harvey family, he thought he should go to the house and look into the matter.

Reverend Harvey later reported:

> I met Mr. Harvey, Mrs. Harvey and their daughter Lillian and talked some time with them. Everything seemed thoroughly satisfactory; his family seemed to know nothing of the arrest, and Mr. Harvey talked as usual, except that I thought he seemed uneasy and fidgety … the whole family spoke of their intention to attend my mission meeting … it was nearly ten o'clock when I left the house.

Reverend Harvey told Chief Randall that he had just been to William Harvey's house and had spoken with Harvey; he didn't think there was cause for concern. Nonetheless, Randall went to Harvey's house to inquire about the gun.

Harvey told Randall the same thing he had told Kickley. He didn't want the embarrassment of having to surrender the gun to the police; the gossip about his difficulties with Lyon had been humiliation enough. He said he would return the gun to Bond on his way to court. Regrettably, Randall accepted this. Like Kickley and Reverend Harvey, the chief was taken in by Harvey's calm and courteous manner. Randall also left without the gun. This would be the worst mistake of his career. But, as he testified later, "If I took the pistol from Harvey without a warrant, I would be open to an action."

William Harvey was a very proud man. Despite his education, he had known extreme poverty and he had lost children to disease; now he had been caught embezzling from a generous and trusting employer. There was probably no doubt in Harvey's mind that he would go to jail for it. The shame might have been more than he could bear. And what about his wife and children? Not only would they have to endure his disgrace, they also would be condemned to a life of want and privation.

Harvey saw only one way out: to spare his loved ones from suffering social ostracism and all the privations of poverty because of his crime, he would kill them. He would do it out of love! Better death than a life of misery. He would send them to heaven, though by doing so he damned himself to hell.

The police later pieced together the sequence of events that took place at the Harvey house after Chief Randall left.

Directly across Woolwich Street from the Harvey residence was a private school run by Miss Alice Hayward. Geraldine was enrolled in the school and was there that morning. Sometime between eleven and twelve o'clock, Harvey sent Lillian, who was now about eighteen, across to the school to borrow a sheet of Easter music. Alice Hayward was busy with her class, but her mother met Lillian and fetched her the music. In the few minutes that Lillian was out of the house, Harvey went into the clothes room where Matilda was and shot her in the back of the head. Lillian returned and went into a back bedroom. Harvey followed her, and murdered her with a shot to the head.

Harvey then went across the street to Miss Hayward's school. Once again, it was Mrs. Hayward who came to the door. Harvey calmly told her he had to take twelve-year-old Geraldine home. He did not give a reason, but the schoolteacher's mother saw no reason not to let the child go with her father. In a front bedroom of the stone house, Harvey shot his youngest child in the back of the head. None of the neighbours heard a thing.

Now only Willie was left, and he was in Toronto. Harvey locked the door as he left the house. He did not go to the Guelph train station where he would be seen and recognized; someone would likely think he was trying to get out of town to avoid his court appearance. Instead, Harvey walked along the railway tracks to Hespeler, about fifteen miles away. (A thirteen-year-old boy named James Smith, who had sometimes run errands for Harvey, saw him on the tracks between Liverpool and Suffolk streets and wondered why he wasn't at work.) In Hespeler, Harvey hired a horse and wagon and drove to Galt. He switched rigs there, and drove another six miles to Harrisburg, where he caught the 6:20 p.m. train to Toronto.

It was that simple! Harvey had the gun, with two bullets in the cylinder, in his pocket. He would kill Willie and then he would kill himself. All of his children would escape the consequences of their father's mistakes.

While Harvey was making his roundabout trip to Toronto, people were waiting for him at the Guelph courthouse. The only person who was concerned that he might try to leave town was Lyon, who kept an eye on the train station just in case. When Harvey failed to appear by 1:30, Chief Randall sent a constable to get him. The policeman returned and said that the house was locked and no one had answered the door.

Lyon immediately posted a $50 reward for information on Harvey's whereabouts. Randall sent messages to police departments across Ontario and beyond, advising them that William H. Harvey was wanted on a charge of embezzlement. Then he went to the Harvey house again, this time accompanied by a Constable Hammond.

When again no one answered the door, Randall forced open the dining room window and climbed in. The house was quiet, but nothing seemed out of order. Randall began a room-by-room search: the dining room, the sitting room, the parlour, the main floor bedroom. Nothing! Then he went upstairs.

On the floor of the closet in the front bedroom, Randall saw something so shocking and so completely unexpected that, as he later put it, he was almost "unmanned." There, lying face-down with a bullet hole in the back of her head, her long hair soaked with blood, was Geraldine Harvey. When the Chief turned the little girl over he heard a gasp and a gurgling noise, and thought for a moment she was still alive. But it was only air escaping from the body. Nonetheless, the shaken Chief placed a pillow under the dead child's head, and continued his search.

In the upstairs back bedroom, Randall found Lillian's body. She was in a crouched position, wedged between the bed and a wall that was smeared with her blood. Even for the veteran policeman, this was beyond belief. Two murders! Dreading what he would find next, Randall went back downstairs to the kitchen. It was evident someone had been in the midst of baking a cake. Randall found Matilda's body on the floor of the clothes room. None of the murder scenes showed any signs of struggle, though it appeared that Geraldine had been trying to hide in the closet. A tear-soaked handkerchief was clutched in Matilda's hand, but no one would ever know why.

Randall went outside and ordered a boy who was passing by on horseback to fetch a doctor immediately. Within minutes Dr. Henry O. Howitt was at the house. He was soon joined by the Wellington County Coroner, Dr. George S. Herod. They confirmed that all three victims had been killed that morning.

It did not take long for the terrible news to race through the community. Soon a crowd of disbelieving Guelphites gathered outside the house at the corner of Woolwich and Edwin streets. Even those who were not personally acquainted with Harvey had often seen him walking through town hand in hand with Geraldine. It didn't seem possible that such a quiet, inoffensive man could commit so horrific a crime. Already the gossip mills were churning out the story that Harvey had been driven to insanity because of the embezzlement charge. The "unfortunate man," as people were calling him, would not otherwise have done the foul deed. Before Harvey could even be located, people were pointing at Lyon as the author of the tragedy.

Now Chief Randall had another, more urgent message to send to other police departments: William Harvey was wanted for murder. At about the same time, Reverend George Harvey sent a telegram to Willie Harvey in Toronto, telling the teenager only that, because of a serious family problem, he must come to Guelph on the first train he could catch. Willie received the telegram at his boarding house, and left Toronto by train at about the time his father was arriving in Harrisburg.

By this time, the Toronto Police knew that the Guelph Police wanted Harvey for both embezzlement and murder. Detective William R. Black was put on the case. A native of Ireland, twenty-nine-year-old Black was a tall, powerfully built man who had joined the Toronto Police

Department in 1884 and had been promoted to the rank of acting detective in just three years. His superiors considered him an officer of great promise. Black went to Willie's boarding house at 25 Grosvenor Street on the possibility that Harvey would try to contact the boy. The landlady told Black that Willie had left in a hurry to catch the six o'clock train to Guelph. However, after Willie's hasty departure, she had received a handwritten message on an official railway form. It was Harvey's message for Willie to meet him at the corner of Yonge and King.

Following Harvey's own instructions, Detective Black went to the intersection. He saw a man pacing up and down, smoking a cigar, and looking up the street as though expecting someone. Certain he had found the suspect wanted for murder in Guelph, Black called to a constable named Leonard who was patrolling nearby. They crossed the street and seized Harvey before he knew what was happening. Constable Leonard kept a firm grip on Harvey's wrist while Black reached into his coat pocket and took out the gun. Harvey did not resist. He only pleaded, "Don't haul me along."

The *Mercury* called the arrest "one of the sharpest pieces of police work in our police history." Detective Black would be praised in the press for, "his clever capture of Harvey, the Guelph murderer."

Harvey spent the night in a Toronto jail cell. In his pockets, the police found the box of cartridges, four cigars, some pencils, a few business letters, a railway timetable, some keys, and $28.98. He sat in silent dejection, refusing to answer questions. He was kept under constant watch in case he attempted suicide.

Back in Guelph, Reverend Harvey met Willie at the train station. He took the boy to the home of a family friend, and told him the sad news. For some time, Willie was stunned and seemed uncomprehending. A rumour circulated that he had taken leave of his senses.

The following morning Chief Randall went to Toronto by train and brought Harvey back to Guelph. The prisoner was just as silent and morose with Randall as he had been with the Toronto police. It would be days before he so much as said a word. A crowd had gathered at the station to see him get off the 2:30 train from Toronto in Randall's custody. To their dismay, the train rolled past the station and stopped behind city hall. Hundreds of men, women, and children raced down the street in hopes of getting a glimpse of the alleged murderer. Only a few had a quick look. Shackled, disheveled, and dazed, Harvey was carried off the train by police officers who bundled him inside and out of sight.

The Coroner's inquest began within an hour. It was still officially in session on Thursday, March 28, 1889, when Matilda, Lillian, and Geraldine were buried in Woodlawn Cemetery. Schools and businesses were closed, and 3,000 people filed past the coffins in St. George's Church. On April 2 the Coroner's jury returned a verdict of willful murder. Harvey would stand trial for his life in the Wellington County Fall Assizes in October 1889.

In Guelph, people were of divided opinions. Many believed Harvey had been driven insane by the circumstances surrounding his arrest for embezzlement. How else could such a gentle, God-fearing Christian husband and father murder his beloved family? The people who held this view were shocked and saddened by the brutal crime, but they saw Harvey as an unfortunate wretch who was to be pitied. In Guelph homes and work places, and on the street corners, those who sympathized with "the poor man" blamed Lyon. They said Lyon had acted too hastily in taking the matter to the police. Had it not been for Lyon's legal action, they argued, Harvey would not have gone crazy and committed the terrible deeds.

Lyon heard these stories and wrote a letter, which appeared in the *Mercury* two days after the murders. He defended his actions, stating:

> I had trusted Mr. Harvey with the entire charge of my books and cash and most of my securities, and it was a severe shock to me to make the unfortunate discovery … Fault has also been found with me for having offered a reward. When the Police Magistrate told me that Mr. Harvey had gone, telegrams were sent to stop him, and I thought that I would by advertising a reward aid the police in bringing him back. At that time the fact of the murders had not transpired. If those who are inclined to find some fault with me would only put themselves in my place, I think they would

see that throughout I only acted as a reasonable man would act according to my knowledge and information. No man can regret more than I do, the dreadful tragedy that has occurred. No one can say that I, or any other person, could possibly have foreseen it.

Lyon's observation that Harvey's crime was completely unpredictable seemed to support the view that the man was insane when he killed his wife and daughters. But other people in Guelph did not think Harvey had lost his mind. A madman, they argued, could not have coolly thought out the plan to kill his wife and daughters one-by-one, and then travel to Toronto by a circuitous route to kill his son

There was even a rumour that alcohol was involved, though it was well-known that Harvey was a teetotaler. The "wets" and the "drys" in Guelph were tied up in a debate over the Scott Act, a temperance law of that time. A story began, allegedly from among the ranks of the "drys," that Harvey had downed a glass of whiskey that fatal morning and had become so crazed from the demon drink that he had slaughtered his innocent family. The wild stories and arguments continued throughout the time leading up to the trial. As the *Mercury* reported, "No one talks of anything else."

Meanwhile, Harvey had emerged from his silent fog. He talked with his jailers, and was a cooperative prisoner. He spent long hours with his new spiritual advisor, Archdeacon Alexander Dixon of St. George's Church. As far as the murders were concerned, Harvey said he could not remember anything about them.

When Harvey's personal belongings were auctioned off to pay his debts, he asked only that he be allowed to keep a few books. He also requested that the money left over, once his accounts had been settled, be given to Willie. Harvey spent much of his time writing letters to the son he had so recently planned to kill.

The fall assizes for Wellington County opened on October 28, but William Harvey's case did not come up until the afternoon of Wednesday, October 30. To the spectators in the crowded courtroom Harvey seemed cool and unconcerned as he pleaded not guilty to the murder charges.

Justice Street presided. E.F.B. Johnston prosecuted for the Crown, assisted by Wellington County Crown Attorney Henry W. Peterson. Leading counsel for the defence was W.M. Lount, Q.C., of Toronto. He was assisted by another Toronto lawyer, G.W. Linderly, and a Guelph lawyer named K. Maclean.

The defence did not deny that Harvey had fired the fatal shots. Their basic argument was that Harvey had been insane when he committed the murders, and therefore not legally responsible for his actions. They produced witnesses —Harvey's friends and colleagues — who testified that when under stress, Harvey was prone to emotional outbreaks and confusion. They all swore to his genuine affection for his family. They believed he couldn't have committed the murders if he had been in his right mind.

Willie, who was clearly uncomfortable on the witness stand, described Harvey as a good and loving father. He said his father wrote to him regularly when he was away in Toronto. Willie produced some of the letters for the court. One of them, dated February 6, 1889, had a touching postscript written by Geraldine. Willie testified that his father was sometimes despondent to the point of illness. In fact, on Willie's last visit home, William had been unable to walk with him to the train station as usual. Fear that his theft might be found out had left Harvey on the verge of a nervous breakdown.

Dr. Stephen Lett, who had posted bail for Harvey after his arrest for embezzlement, was an *alienist*, the nineteenth-century term for psychiatrist. Before coming to Guelph to establish the Homewood Retreat, he had worked in asylums in Amherstburg and Hamilton. At that time, Dr. Lett was one of Ontario's foremost experts on mental illness, and had examined Harvey after he'd been brought back from Toronto.

Dr. Lett testified that, at the time of the murders, Harvey had been in an "anergic stupor"; a form of insanity in which his mind went blank and rendered him unaccountable for his actions. When Harvey killed his wife and daughters, Lett said, he was in the grip of a homicidal mania. In Lett's opinion, Harvey had truly been under the delusion that he was doing the best thing for his loved ones by killing them to spare them from shame and poverty. Three other mental-illness experts agreed with Dr. Lett: Dr.

Charles Clarke, from the Asylum for the Insane in Kingston; Dr. Daniel Clarke, the medical superintendent from the Ontario Asylum in Toronto; and his colleague, Dr. Joseph Workman, who had been superintendent of the Ontario Asylum from 1853 to 1875.

The medical evidence given by these four men was challenged by Dr. Herod, who, in addition to being the county coroner, was also the physician for the Guelph Gaol. While he was not an alienist, he based his opinions on his observations of Harvey during his incarceration. As far as Dr. Herod was concerned, Harvey knew exactly what he was doing when he fired the shots. Moreover, he said that no insane man could have plotted the devious route Harvey used to get out of Guelph and then travel to Toronto where he attempted to lure his son into an ambush. To support Dr. Herod's testimony, the Crown called upon two "expert" witnesses: Dr. James H. Richardson, the physician for the Toronto Gaol; and Dr. W.T. Aikens, the physician at the Central Prison in Toronto. They were medical doctors with "some experience in insanity." They testified that Harvey did not suffer from any form of mental illness, and that he was aware that he was doing great wrong when he committed the murders.

In his closing address, Lount pleaded with the jury to find Harvey not guilty by reason of insanity. He said that everything about Harvey's actions clearly showed that he should be sent not to the gallows, but to an asylum for the rest of his life. "God only knows whether or not the last is the heaviest," he said in conclusion.

Prosecutor Johnston made an equally strong argument for the jury to find Harvey sane and guilty. He insisted that while Harvey might have been depressed and of a strange temperament, he was not mentally ill. The jury retired and took only an hour to reach a unanimous verdict: "We find the prisoner guilty." Justice Street sentenced Harvey to hang on November 29. He left it up to the condemned man to choose the time of day.

Harvey barely blinked as the death sentence was pronounced. One reporter noted, "It was apparent that he had nerves of steel." In fact, Harvey had expected the verdict and had resigned himself to his fate. He had requested in advance that he not be hanged on certain dates in December, since they were family anniversaries. His stoicism probably stemmed from the relief of knowing that it would be all over before the end of November.

William Harvey was a condemned man, but the legal battle was not over. Many people were outraged over the conviction and the sentence. Archdeacon Dixon sent an angry letter to the newspapers in which he severely criticized the outcome of the trial. The letter denounced the men of the jury as illiterates who obviously did not understand the medical testimony. "Suppose there was a great financial question at stake, would such a jury be tolerated for a moment?" he asked. "But this is only a case of life and death!"

The *Mercury* responded with an editorial stating that Harvey had received a fair trial and deserved his fate. The *Mercury* congratulated the prosecutor and the jury on a job well done. The *Toronto Globe* got into the fray by taking up the argument that Harvey was obviously insane, thus touching off a war of words with the *Mercury*. The Harvey case became an issue of heated debate across the country.

Harvey's friends circulated a petition to have the death sentence commuted to life imprisonment. In just eight days it gathered 3,270 signatures from thirty-four communities across Canada. On November 19 a small group travelled to Ottawa to meet the Minister of Justice, Sir John Thompson (the future prime minister of Canada). Besides the petition, they had a letter from H.W. Peterson, one of the lawyers who had prosecuted Harvey, stating that he and the community at large would be satisfied that justice had been served if Harvey went to prison for life. Thompson considered the matter for a week before denying the request. In the Guelph Gaol, Sheriff Robert McKim didn't have the stomach to tell Harvey the bad news himself. He simply handed the prisoner a copy of the *Globe* with the story on the front page.

Sheriff McKim had one more unpleasant job: he had to find an executioner. If he couldn't find someone to hang Harvey, he would be duty-bound to do it himself. Like most Canadian sheriffs, McKim was not willing to play the role of hangman.

McKim advertised for an executioner and received four responses. He selected a twenty-three-year old farm labourer named G. Smith (whose identity was initially kept secret). Smith, who was paid $25 for the job, had never hanged anyone before, but McKim was confident the young man could handle the task. Smith would prove him wrong.

The gallows that had been shipped to Guelph from Toronto was considered a state-of-the-art device. Instead of dropping the prisoner through a trap door in an elevated platform, this gallows used a 300 pound weight which, when it fell, yanked the victim up by the neck. If it worked correctly, the prisoner's neck was broken instantly and death was swift and painless. This "jerk 'em up" method was thought to be more humane than the traditional gallows, because it spared the prisoner the awful ordeal of climbing the stairs of the scaffold.

Two days before the execution date, Willie had a final meeting with his father. Willie had telegraphed Lord Stanley, the governor general of Canada, asking him to intercede on his father's behalf. The governor general replied that, as the queen's representative, he was forbidden to interfere. At their last visit, Harvey and his son spoke for half an hour, and then parted after a tearful embrace. Willie got on the first train to Toronto. He did not want to be in Guelph on the day of the execution.

William Harvey spent November 28, his last day on earth, writing letters and reading his Bible. After supper, he spent an hour in prayer with Archdeacon Dixon. That night, a guard named Doughty asked Harvey for a memento. Harvey gave him his ivory cuff buttons, saying, "Don't hawk these things round and show them to everybody. I don't like that sort of thing. I have nothing else I can give you. If you want an inch of the rope, you will have to ask the hangman for it." (After an execution it was common for the hangman to chop the rope into small pieces and sell them as souvenirs.)

Meanwhile, young Mr. Smith was apparently having second thoughts about the ghastly task he had to perform. Sheriff McKim lodged him in a jail cell for the night, under the guard's watch in case he tried to run away: Smith had agreed to hang Harvey, and the sheriff had no intentions of letting him out of it.

Harvey had chosen eight o'clock in the morning as the hour of his death. On his final night he went to bed at 10:30 but slept fitfully. He got up before five o'clock, and had some toast and coffee. Archdeacon Dixon and a colleague, Reverend G. B. Cook, arrived just before seven o'clock to provide spiritual support; and Sheriff McKim came to the cell at 7:45. Harvey showed him his left hand. Around the two middle fingers, he had secured two pieces of paper. One was a note about a birthday, written by Geraldine. The other was a letter of forgiveness Willie had given him. Ten minutes later the hangman arrived.

Smith pinioned Harvey's arms. The procession to the gallows began just before eight o'clock. Reverend Cook led the way, followed by Dixon in his cassock. Harvey walked behind him, with McKim on one side and a guard on the other. Smith was last in line.

About seventy witnesses waited in the snow-covered jail yard. Because of a federal-government ruling in 1869, hangings in Canada were no longer public affairs that drew crowds of spectators. Executions were carried out behind the walls of county jails, and only people with official invitations — newspaper reporters, court officials, jail personnel, and a few selected private citizens — were allowed to watch the gruesome spectacle. Police prevented people from watching from rooftops overlooking the jail yard. Nonetheless, some men and boys climbed trees to get a good look at the proceedings, and disturbed the solemnity of the occasion with what the *Mercury* called "heartless laughter."

Harvey showed no fear when he stood beneath the rope. Sheriff McKim asked him if he had any statement to make. Harvey replied, "I have not."

The hangman pulled a black hood over Harvey's head and fastened a strap around his legs. Harvey obligingly lifted his chin as Smith slipped the noose over his head and tightened it around his neck. Smith stepped back, and Dixon began to recite the Lord's Prayer. At the words, "Thy will be done," Smith suddenly cut the rope holding the 300-pound weight.

The execution of William Harvey would go down as one of the most badly botched legal hangings in Canadian history. Instead of setting the knot behind Harvey's left ear, the amateur Smith put it under his chin. When the weight dropped, Harvey shot up into the air and then dropped until the rope snapped taut, leaving him dangling a foot-and-a-half above the ground. He was alive and slowly strangling. As the horrified witnesses looked on, Harvey kicked and jerked. He tried to pull his hands free of their bonds. The witnesses heard groans and choking sounds come from the black hood.

A full seven minutes after the hangman had dropped the weight, Dr. Herod stepped onto a chair beside the dangling man and checked for a pulse. Harvey's heart was still beating. Herod put his hand into Harvey's, and, to the coroner's dismay, the dying man clutched it tightly. Three more long minutes passed before the twitching and groaning finally stopped, and Herod pronounced Harvey dead. The witnesses fled from the jail yard in disgust.

At Sheriff McKim's request, Harvey's body wasn't buried in the jail yard, as was usually done with executed murderers. It was interred with those of his victims in Woodlawn Cemetery under a stone slab that simply read, "Harvey." The *Globe* said of the hanging:

> The cruel deed is done. The murder of three helpless women was atoned by W.H. Harvey in the gaol yard here this morning. He died like a stoic, but was hanged like a dog. The law has been satisfied but humanity was outraged by the shocking bungling of the youthful hangman. Long may it be again before those whom duty compels them to witness public executions will be called upon to view the excruciating contortions of a human being forced out of this world by the machinery of the law.

In a Canadian court of law today, William Harvey would certainly be found not guilty by reason of insanity, and committed to an institution. Dr. Lett's expertise in diseases of the mind would outweigh Dr. Herod's lack of it. In fact, just before the execution, Archdeacon Dixon was interviewed by the *Globe*. He told the Toronto reporter of a conversation he'd had with Harvey:

> He [Harvey] suffered indescribable mental torture all night previous to the death of his beloved ones. He could not sleep, and as he looked on his wife beside him his anguish was horrible. He bought the pistol for the purpose of suicide, but as he walked the street he thought of the warning given

him of the dangerous effect which a shock would have on his wife. Then he imagined the poverty his daughters would be plunged in by his own removal and the possible death of the mother. Here ended his consciousness of free action.

The tragic story of the Harvey murders was the inspiration for Guelph author Mary Swan's 2008 novel *The Boys in the Trees*.

# 5.

# THE HESLOP MURDER:
## THIEVES IN THE NIGHT

By January of 1891, when he was in his eightieth year, John Heslop was one of the most respected men in Ancaster Township, near Hamilton, Ontario. He had a fine stone house on Mineral Springs Road, in a somewhat isolated location. He was a prosperous farmer, and Treasurer of the Township. He was a man of both strong will and strong convictions.

Heslop was born in Cumberland, England, in 1812. In 1815 his family emigrated to North America. After sojourns in New Brunswick, Baltimore, Washington, D.C., and Virginia, the Heslop family settled in Ancaster in 1829. In the Rebellion of 1837–38, young John Heslop supported William Lyon Mackenzie. He carried messages for the rebels, and personally escorted Mackenzie through Ancaster during the tumultuous time of the insurrection. When the uprising failed, and British troops were rounding up Mackenzie sympathizers, Heslop somehow managed to avoid arrest. His name did not appear on the lists of men wanted for "treason." For the rest of his life, Heslop kept letters he had received from Mackenzie as his prized possessions.

After the rebellion, Heslop settled back into the life of a farmer, and he did well for himself. In 1844 he was married. From 1853 until 1858 he was Warden of Wentworth County. In 1862 he built his stone house. In 1872 he was appointed treasurer of the township, a position he held until the day he died. Ironically, it was that honour that would lead to his death.

At about 1:30 a.m. on January 27, 1891, John Heslop and his wife Elizabeth were asleep in a second floor bedroom of their house on Mineral Springs Road. Their forty-five-year-old daughter, Sara, slept in the next bedroom. All three were jarred awake by a loud crash downstairs. Still quite agile for a man of seventy-nine, Heslop leapt out of bed and told Elizabeth to light a candle. He dashed out to the hallway in his nightshirt and called, "Who's there?"

A gruff voice replied, "Go back to bed."

Elizabeth came out of the bedroom with a candle at the same time that Sara emerged from her room. In the flickering light the Heslops saw two men groping their way up the stairs. Their faces were hidden by cloth masks. The burglars had smashed in the back door to enter the house. Elizabeth's candle went out. She and Heslop retreated to their bedroom.

John Heslop, a former rebel, was not going to be intimidated by a pair of masked thieves. When Elizabeth relit her candle, Heslop seized a chair, but forgot all about the loaded gun he had hidden in the room.

Heslop dashed out with the chair raised high. He went down the stairs, straight at the nearest intruder, and smashed the chair over the man's head. The wooden chair broke into pieces and the burglar crumpled, his head bleeding. The second intruder suddenly pulled out a .32 calibre revolver. Without a word of warning he shot Heslop from point blank range. The bullet struck Heslop in the left breast and severed an artery near his heart. Without uttering a sound, Heslop collapsed, rolled down a few steps to the bottom of the stairway, and lay still. He was dead. Not much more than a minute had passed since the thieves had smashed in the back door.

Elizabeth and Sara screamed. The gunman told them the old man would be all right. Then he demanded money. The burglars had assumed that because Heslop was the township treasurer, there would be money in his house.

By now the robber with the bloodied head was back on his feet. A terrified Elizabeth told the burglars, who reeked of whiskey, that there was no money. Sara tried to go to her father, but the robbers prevented her. They pushed both women into a bedroom and warned them that there were four men watching the house. Once again, they demanded money. Elizabeth insisted that there was no money in the house.

The gunman replied angrily, "I know a damned sight better! There is township money in this house, and we are going to have it!"

"If you think so, you may go and search for it," Elizabeth wept.

The gunman gave his pistol to his injured partner and told him to watch the women while he ransacked the house. He found no money: Heslop's safe was empty. The thieves got nothing but a few pieces of cheap jewelry. They even overlooked Elizabeth's purse, which had about $40 in it.

When the two men finally left, the women heard the sound of a rig driving away. They knelt over Heslop, but detected no signs of life. His nightshirt was still smoldering from the flash of gunpowder. The Heslops had a hired man named John Reading who lived in quarters about two hundred yards from the main house. Sara ran there and told him what had happened. Reading immediately dashed off to Ancaster to fetch a doctor, and to inform the local constable, a man named Crann.

The doctor could do nothing but pronounce John Heslop dead. Because there had been a light snowfall, Constable Crann was able to follow the tracks the bandits' rig had made. They went straight to Ancaster, and then on to Hamilton where they were lost in the muck and slush of city traffic.

Hamilton police scoured the city for several days, looking for any information that might lead them to Heslop's killers. They didn't have much to go on. Footprints in the snow around the Heslop house indicated that four men had participated in the crime. The police questioned a few passing tramps, but released them. The offer of a $700 reward for information produced no results.

Oliver Mowat, the Premier of Ontario (and also Attorney General), sent Provincial Government Detective William Greer to take over the case. Greer was a veteran police officer with a solid reputation as an investigator. He immediately began to chase down leads that took him from Toronto to Rochester, New York, and Chicago. All of which led to dead ends. After several fruitless weeks, John Heslop's many friends began to fear that the killers would never be found.

Then Greer heard rumours that three ne'er-do-wells from the Brantford area had been seen in Ancaster in the last week of January. Two of them, Samuel Goosey and George Douglas, were from the Six Nations Reserve. Goosey was a known livestock thief. Douglas was currently wanted on

*Hamilton Spectator*

Artist's version of the murder of John Heslop. Actually, only two robbers entered the house, and they were masked. Heslop was wearing his nightshirt.

suspicion of stealing harnesses. The third man was Jack Bartram. He was white, fifty-four years old, and lived in nearby Middleport. All three had reputations as ruffians. They had all been in jail several times for theft and public drunkenness.

Bartram had actually gained notoriety as a local desperado. He was reputed to be "the hardest man on the Grand River," and had been imprisoned for rustling cattle. He had also shot and wounded a man, but had somehow managed to avoid prosecution for that. Later investigations would reveal that Jack Bartram had been the leader of an outlaw gang that terrorized the Brantford district in the 1870s. For a while his gang had robbed at will. People were afraid to go to the police out of fear of having their barns and homes torched. The Bartram gang even got away with stealing an entire herd of sheep.

The gang's activity declined quickly after a Native woman shot one of them when they tried to break into her house. A police agent infiltrated the bunch, and several of them were sent to prison. But the law didn't get Jack Bartram.

By this time Bartram was getting old for the hard life of an outlaw, but he continued to operate as a lone bandit. It wasn't easy, because a cancerous growth on his face just below his right eye made him easily identifiable. He had spent some years in the United States, where he was wanted on several criminal charges. New York State police actually told Detective Greer that Bartram was one of the worst hoodlums on their wanted list. Surprisingly, Bartram had several children who had never been in trouble with the law. His daughters taught school in Michigan.

Detective Greer learned that Goosey and Douglas often went to the Tuscarora Reservation near Lewiston, New York, where they allegedly had connections. He went there on a fact-finding expedition, and instructed the Brantford police to watch for Bartram. In December of 1891, Greer saw Goosey and Douglas in Lewiston. He did not have enough evidence to have them legally arrested and extradited, so he resorted to trickery.

Douglas and Goosey were heavy drinkers, and were well known in establishments that catered to Natives. Greer arranged for a bartender to slip each of them an old-fashioned knockout drink known as a Mickey Finn. While the two were in a drugged stupor, Greer had them ferried across to the Canadian side, and locked in the Niagara Falls jail. Greer's actions were completely illegal, but he had a murder to solve, and police didn't always observe the finer points of the law when Natives were involved.

When Goosey and Douglas awoke, surprised to find themselves in a Canadian jail, Greer told them that he was taking them to Brantford on theft charges (omitting the detail about them being murder suspects). Meanwhile, he'd been informed that Bartram had been seen near Middleton. Greer sent instructions for the outlaw to be arrested on charges of livestock theft, but not to be told anything about the Heslop case.

Bartram was drunk when he was apprehended by Constable P.C. Adams of the Brantford Police Department. Bartram told the officer, "Look here, now! You've got me solid, but if you will leave off on this charge of cattle stealing, I will give you some good pointers about the fellows who murdered old man Heslop at Ancaster last winter."

"I won't let you off," Adams replied. "You must come to Brantford jail with me."

"Well, when we get there, you tell them that I know who killed the old man, and will give the whole thing away if they will only let me go."

But when they arrived at the jail, Bartram changed his tune. He said he knew nothing about the murder. Goosey and Douglas soon arrived at the Brantford jail, where they learned of Bartram's offer to tell the police everything he knew about the Heslop murder. They began to have similar thoughts.

A *Toronto Globe* reporter went to the Brantford jail to interview Bartram, and found the prisoner in a foul mood. Bartram asked the journalist what he wanted. The reporter replied, "Oh, I like to see you boys in hard luck comfortable."

"You do, eh?" Bartram grunted. "Well, I wish I was as comfortable as you, and I would not stay in this hell hole long."

News of the arrests spread, and people crowded the streets outside the Brantford jail, anxious to get a look at the prisoners. Officially, Bartram, Goosey, and Douglas were charged with theft. But everybody knew the real reason they were in jail: Bartram was suspected of shooting John Heslop, and Goosey and Douglas were likely his accomplices. It was generally agreed that if ever there was a villain low enough to shoot down an elderly man and terrorize two helpless women, it was Jack Bartram. There was also speculation over who would get the reward, which had grown to the incredible sum of $2,000!

Goosey and Douglas knew that if they were convicted of being accomplices to murder, they could hang along with the man who had actually pulled the trigger. To save their own necks, and perhaps thinking they would be eligible for the reward money, they decided to turn Queen's evidence. That meant they would be granted immunity from prosecution in return for testifying for the Crown.

The pair spoke to the police, and implicated a fourth suspect, Jack Lottridge. He was about thirty and had never been in trouble for anything more serious than public drunkenness. But Lottridge was Jack Bartram's nephew! The constables who picked Lottridge up told him he was being subpoenaed on the theft charges against his uncle. When he arrived at the jail and learned he was a suspect in the Heslop murder case, he almost fainted.

The prisoners were taken to Hamilton to await trial at the next assizes. Elizabeth and Sara Heslop went to Hamilton, but were unable to identify any of the suspects because the men who had broken into their home were masked. (Elizabeth never did recover from the shock of her husband's murder. In February of 1892 she fell ill and died at the age of seventy-two.)

According to the story Goosey and Douglas told the police, they had been associated with Bartram and Lottridge for years. The day before the murder the four men met at Lottridge's house. They were drinking and playing dominoes when Bartram suddenly announced that he knew where they could steal four or five hundred dollars. The others were immediately interested. They had a few more drinks, and then got into a wagon and headed for Ancaster. They made one stop to share a bottle of whiskey Bartram had brought along. By the time they reached the gate of the Heslop house it was late. Goosey and Douglas told the police they had never been to the house before, and did not know who lived there.

The gang drove part way up the lane, then stopped and got out of the wagon. Bartram told Lottridge to stay with the horse while he and the others went to the house. The front door was locked, so they went around to the back. The door there was locked, too. Bartram was trying to pick the lock when Goosey said, "Move back, and I will open it for you."

Using a piece of cordwood as a battering ram, Goosey broke the door open. Bartram and Douglas donned masks and went inside. Goosey stood guard outside. When the robbers confronted Heslop on the stairs, the old man struck Douglas with the chair. Bartram was the only one carrying a gun, and he shot Heslop.

When Goosey heard the gunshot, he said that he'd panicked. He ran to where Lottridge was holding the horse and told him that the others had either shot somebody or had been shot. Lottridge said, "Jump in and let us go. If they have shot anybody, we will all hang for it!"

The two drove about a quarter of a mile down the road before Goosey regained his composure and turned the wagon around. They arrived back at the gate just as Bartram and Douglas came out of the house. Lottridge asked if anybody had been hurt, and Bartram answered no. They piled into the wagon and fled through Ancaster as fast as they could. Bartram had said, "I'll bet that fellow won't hit anyone with a chair again."

Bartram told the others that he had taken some jewelry, which he would sell and then divide the money. At about dawn, he dropped the other men off to walk the rest of the way home while he drove the wagon to Hamilton. He warned them to say nothing to anyone.

That, at least, was the version Goosey and Douglas provided. It seemed to fit the evidence the police had already gathered. Jack Bartram was formally charged with the murder of John Heslop, and Jack Lottridge with being an accessory.

The trial was held in Hamilton in March of 1892. It was a sensation, lasting nine days. Hamiltonians actually held murder trial parties. The courtroom was jammed every day, and reporters who didn't arrive early enough to take their seats near the front of the room were physically passed, hand-by-hand, over the heads of the spectators. People still out in the street nearly rioted when told they wouldn't be admitted. Newspapers commented disapprovingly on the large number of "the fairer sex" in attendance. After all, a murder trial was no place for women!

Before the trial had even begun, an editorial in the *Hamilton Herald* stated, "The hangman's knot begins to loom up in the distance." Several times during the trial Justice Rose, the presiding magistrate, complained about the sensationalism the press was creating. He threatened to have certain newspapers charged with contempt. The editor of the *Hamilton Spectator* joked about his "boys" being put on bread and water."

The prosecutor was John Crerar, Crown Attorney for Wentworth County. Louis Heyd was defence counsel for Jack Bartram, and T.W. Nesbitt for Jack Lottridge. A total of 116 witnesses would be called by the Crown and the defence. Many of the witnesses were from the Six Nations Reserve near Brantford, and the Tuscarora Reservation near Lewiston. This caused a problem with translation, since some of the witnesses only spoke Tuscarora, but the official Native interpreter from the Six Nations Reserve spoke Mohawk. Newspaper reports revealed the racist attitudes of the time: Native women were called "Minehahas," Native men were "bucks," and reporters commented on how some of the Native witnesses "actually" seemed to be intelligent.

The Crown based its case on the story Goosey and Douglas had told the police. Their statement was supported by men who had been prisoners in the Brantford jail with Bartram and Lottridge. One man said he had heard Lottridge offer Douglas fifty dollars to keep his mouth shut. Another claimed to have heard Bartram say, "My God! If Jack Lottridge says ten words, then I'm a goner sure!" The police had put an ex-convict named Michael Mandible in the cells as a "secret service man." He testified that he had heard Bartram talking about the robbery and the murder.

However, under cross-examination Goosey and Douglas stumbled several times. They disagreed on how many of the gang had masks. They contradicted each other on where Goosey had found the piece of cordwood he used on the door. They weren't even sure how many pieces of cordwood had been used. Small points, to be sure, but the defence pounced on them.

Then Heyd and Nesbitt produced alibis for their clients. Fanny Dinsmore, Lottridge's sister and Bartram's niece, testified that at the time of the murder her brother was at home asleep. "Uncle Jack," she said, was preparing to deliver a load of cordwood and hay to Hamilton. Several other witnesses, including Bartram's son, supported her testimony.

The defence revealed that Detective Greer and other police officers had plied Natives on both reservations with liquor to get information. Heyd and Nesbitt also produced witnesses who testified that at the time Goosey and Douglas were supposed to have been drinking with Bartram and Lottridge, they were actually at the Six Nations Reserve attending the funeral of a woman named Katie White. This became one of the most fiercely argued points in the trial. Some of the witnesses from the reserve said Goosey and Douglas were at the funeral; others said they weren't. (For a long time after the trial it was a standing joke in the region for a person who had to explain an absence, or for a husband who came home late, to say, "I was at Katie White's funeral.")

Nesbitt and Heyd argued that the Crown's "jailbird" witnesses were not trustworthy, while the witnesses for the defence were all upright citizens. Crerar replied that when prosecuting disreputable characters like Jack Bartram, the Crown had to seek witnesses among the lower elements of society, because those were the people with whom such men associated. Crerar did not go so far as to accuse defence witnesses of lying, but suggested that in their desire to protect men who were their relatives or friends, they had confused the dates.

When all the evidence was in, and the Crown and defence had made their final statements, Justice Rose very carefully gave his instructions to the jury. The twelve men retired behind closed doors. Three and a half hours later they sent word that they had reached a unanimous verdict.

As the jurymen filed back into the courtroom, Bartram and Lottridge sat in silence. Throughout the trial Lottridge had been nervous and jumpy. Now, with the prospect of the noose in front of him, he was a bundle of barely restrained tension. Bartram, the hard case, looked pale. Justice Rose was writing something in his judicial notebook as the men of the jury took their seats. The court clerk asked, "Gentlemen of the jury, have you reached a verdict?"

The foreman stood up and said, "Not guilty!"

It was a stunning announcement. No one was more surprised than Justice Rose, who, in anticipation of a verdict of guilty, had just written in his notebook, "The sentence of the court upon you John Lottridge and John Bartram is that you …" The next words would have been the ones that condemned the two men to hang.

Goosey and Douglas were released. Lottridge went to jail for burglary, and Bartram for cattle rustling. Members of the jury explained that in their opinion, too many witnesses had been lying. They couldn't decide who had been telling the truth, and felt they had to give the accused the benefit of the doubt. Nonetheless, rumours circulated that the jury had been bribed.

Sara Heslop lived in the house on Mineral Springs Road until she sold it in 1909. The house, now known as Woodend, is currently the headquarters for the Hamilton Region Conservation Authority. The murder of John Heslop is officially an unsolved Canadian mystery.

# 6.

## HUGH LYNN:
### THE SAVARY ISLAND MURDERS

Savary Island lies in the Strait of Georgia, about 145 kilometres northwest of Vancouver. It is just 8 kilometres long, and less than a kilometre wide. Nicknamed "Canada's Tropical Paradise," Savary Island has sandy beaches that are popular with vacationers. However, in the 1890s, the island was just another isolated spot on the wild British Columbia coast, visited only by hunters and trappers. One autumn night in 1893, it was the setting for an act of violence that led to a controversial murder trial.

In 1886, a sixty-nine-year-old trader named John Green established a trading post on Savary Island. Originally from England, Green had been successful as a farmer and trader, and had followed a gold rush to Virginia City, Nevada. He had first seen Savary Island while trading up and down the British Columbia coast in his sloop, the *Wanderer*.

By 1893, Green, now seventy-six, was well-established on Savary. His compound included a solid, one-room log cabin with an annex, which served as his store, animal shelters, and storage sheds, and another small cabin that he used as an overnight guest house for Native customers. Green raised sheep, pigs, and chickens. The livestock enabled him to add fresh meat and eggs to his inventory of canned food, dry goods, fishing equipment, tobacco, hardware, and ammunition. Quite likely, Green dealt in alcohol.

Green traded with white and Native trappers and hunters for otter, mink, and bear skins, which he then sold to fur dealers. He did very well financially, but he did not trust banks. Instead of depositing his money, he kept it in an iron cash box. Green had once been robbed of several hundred dollars by a thief named Bragg, who then escaped to the United States. Unfortunately, not even that experience convinced him to put his money in a safe place. Local British Columbia Provincial Police constables warned him that he was asking for trouble by keeping a large amount of money on the premises, to no avail.

Because of his age, his terrible arthritis, and the fact that he used two walking sticks to get around, Green needed hired help to assist him with the work. Several men worked for him at different times, but none stayed on for long. That was probably because Green would go on drinking bouts, and when in his cups he tended to get belligerent. With his arthritic pain numbed by whiskey, he no longer needed the canes, and would behave violently. One time, he allegedly attacked a man with an axe, without fatal results. On two other occasions, a drunken Green was said to have shot at people.

Green finally found a hired man who was reliable, and who, evidently, could put up with him when he was on a bender. Tom Taylor was in his late forties, and an old acquaintance of Green's. Green and Taylor worked well together, the trading post prospered, and Green made Taylor a partner. The two men were respected by both their white and Native customers. Green purchased more property on Savary Island, and planned to expand his enterprise. But he never got the chance.

On the morning of October 30, 1893, three men, Norman Smith, Dick Lewis, and Albert Hanson, were travelling up the coast by boat when they made a stop at Savary Island. They were surprised to find no one around, and the door to Green's store locked. They pushed the cabin door open, and were shocked by what they saw.

Old John Green was slumped against the wall behind the door, dead! Tom Taylor's body lay sprawled face down in a pool of blood in the middle of the cabin floor. Both corpses were stiff with rigor mortis, and had shotguns clutched in their hands. It looked like Green and Taylor had killed each other in a gunfight. Oddly, Green was naked from the waist down. His underwear was around his ankles, he had a sock on one foot, and nothing on the other.

While Smith and Lewis remained at the trading post, Hanson sailed to the fishing village of Lund on the mainland to report the deaths. On November 1, the *Stella*, a small steam launch from the town of Comox, arrived at Savary Island. Aboard were Mike Manson, who was both coroner and justice of the peace; Constable Walter Anderson of the BCPP; and a doctor.

The doctor examined the bodies, and determined that the men had been dead since October 26. Anderson immediately deduced that Green and Taylor had not shot each other: their cold, dead hands grasped shotguns, but the wounds had been made by rifle bullets. Green had a bullet wound in his breast, just above his heart. Taylor had been shot in the back. There were bullet holes in the walls, and a dozen or so .44 calibre cartridge casings on the floor. A clock had been smashed by a bullet, and its hands were stopped at 10:10.

Dust and oil in the barrels of the shotguns showed that they had not been fired in a long time, and both guns still had unfired shells in the breeches. Moreover, Taylor's left hand was still holding his pipe: Taylor would have needed both hands to shoot a weapon that kicked like a

Image 1876KB courtesy of Royal BC Museum, BC Archives

John Green's cabin and trading post on Savary Island, where Green and Tom Taylor were killed.

shotgun, and it wasn't likely that he would have been smoking his pipe during a shootout.

The cabin had also obviously been ransacked. The place was littered with six empty whiskey bottles and the stuffing from two torn-up mattresses. Pots and pans, canned goods, the empty and lidless cash box, and an empty leather wallet were strewn about the floor. Whoever was responsible for the killings had probably stripped the pants from Green's body in order to search them for money. Either that, or Green had been shot in cold blood while he was getting undressed for bed. Placing shotguns in the dead men's hands had clearly been a ridiculously inept attempt to disguise an act of robbery and murder.

Crime scene investigation in a frontier region of nineteenth-century Canada was primitive, but Constable Anderson did the best he could with the methods and materials available. He put cedar sticks into the bullet holes in the walls, the clock, and the bodies. From the positions of the sticks, he deduced that the shooter had stood in the centre of the room. Beneath a broken window, Anderson found some spilled bird shot and two plugs of tobacco. He also found another empty whiskey bottle in the guest cabin. Anderson initially thought that the crime had been committed by local Natives during a drunken spree. However, in an interview with Charles Thulin, Lund's co-founder and proprietor of the community's hotel, Anderson first heard about a man named Hugh Lynn.

The son of a British Royal Engineer named John Lynn, for whom Lynn Canyon and Lynn Creek were named, Hugh was born in 1858 aboard the ship transporting his parents to British Columbia. Hughie, as he was known to family and friends, grew up to be a ne'er-do-well. He disliked work, but tried his hand at beachcombing, trapping, and fishing, without much success. He was arrested several times for selling liquor to Natives. In fact, much to the general disapproval of the white community, Hugh Lynn preferred the company of Natives. In 1890 he took a Bella Coola Kimsquit woman named Jenny Que-Ah-Boketo (also called Jenny Botiko) as his common-law wife. Jenny had a four-year-old son named Louis from a previous relationship.

Hugh Lynn's behaviour might not have been entirely due to an indolent nature. People who knew him said he was "an individual of weak and defective mind … little better than half-witted." Fur traders evidently took advantage of him. One trader admitted that he "had never made so much profit" as he did from one purchase of furs he'd made from Lynn.

Charlie Thulin told Walter Anderson that on October 26, John Green and Hugh Lynn were in Lund, drinking. Green paid for the whiskey from a large roll of bills. They left the village, but later that same evening, Lynn came back. He had a note in Green's handwriting ordering six bottles of whiskey. Lynn said that Green had offered him a job at the trading post for the winter, and that Jenny would be doing the cooking. Lynn got back in his boat to return to Savary Island, and that was the last Thulin had seen of him.

Not long after his conversation with Thulin, Anderson met some Natives at Okeover Arm who had seen Hugh Lynn a week earlier. Lynn had been travelling with Jenny and Louis in a fifteen-foot, double-ended red skiff. As far as Anderson could determine, there had been no subsequent sightings of Lynn and his family.

The *Victoria Daily Colonist* had two theories as to what had happened on Savary Island. One theory held that drunken Natives had massacred Green, Taylor, Lynn, Jenny, and Louis, and had buried the bodies of Hughie, the woman, and the boy. The other was that Bragg, the outlaw who had robbed Green once before, had returned from the United States to steal the rest of the money, and that he had done the killing. The paper suggested that Lynn could have been in cahoots with Bragg, but then dismissed the idea. "Lynn bears a bad character generally in the district," the *Colonist* said. "He is, however, a sneak and a coward, and would not be suspected of having embarked in so desperate an enterprise as the island affair seems to have been."

Justice of the Peace Mike Manson held to the idea that Natives had killed Green and Taylor, and possibly Lynn, Jenny, and Louis. Then, just before Christmas, an abandoned skiff was found near Oyster Beach on Vancouver Island. It matched the description of the one Lynn had been using. In it, Anderson found bird shot similar to that which he had picked up under the broken window of Green's trading post.

The skiff's discovery did not necessarily mean that Lynn was still alive, but Jack Bledsoe, an American-born journalist for the Victoria

*Daily Colonist*, believed that the police should be looking into that possibility. Bledsoe had written articles that were critical of how the Provincial Police were handling the Savary Island investigation. Superintendent Fred S. Hussey of the Victoria detachment called Bledsoe into his office. Bledsoe convinced him that Jenny could be the key to tracking down Lynn. In those days, when police manpower was spread thin, it was not uncommon for civilians to be sworn in as temporary special constables, with the legal power to conduct investigations and make arrests. Hussey made Bledsoe a special constable, and put him on the case. Bledsoe began his assignment on January 24, 1894.

First he went to Savary Island to look over the murder scene. Then he made his way by sea, through a howling blizzard, to Jenny's home village at Bella Coola. The people there had not seen Jenny in a long time, but Bledsoe learned that, through an inheritance, she owned some property near Port Townsend in Washington State.

After reporting to Hussey in Victoria, Bledsoe went to Port Townsend. He was told that Jenny hadn't been seen in the area in three years. Bledsoe was certain that if Lynn and Jenny were alive, they would show up there sooner or later. He asked the local police to keep their eyes and ears open, and then returned to Victoria. For four months Bledsoe heard nothing, but then his patience was rewarded.

In April, the Port Townsend police reported that a white man, a Native woman, and a young boy had been seen near Jenny's property. Bledsoe and Superintendent Hussey hurried to Port Townsend on a hired steamer. Their inquiries directed them to Squaw Island. Jenny had a daughter there who was married to a rancher. Lynn, Jenny, and Louis were believed to be staying in the rancher's cabin.

On April 9, Hussey and Bledsoe approached the cabin during a rainstorm accompanied by an American sheriff named Thomas, and a deputy named Delaney. Hussey and Delaney went to the front door, while Bledsoe and Thomas covered the back. Smoke from the chimney told them that someone was home.

Hussey knocked on the door, and a gaunt-looking man answered. Hussey asked for a glass of water, and engaged the man in casual conversation. Then Hussey asked the man's name. "Gallagher," he said. He suddenly became suspicious and moved toward a Winchester rifle that was hanging on a wall. Then he said, "No, it's Newton."

Before the man could reach the gun, Bledsoe and Thomas came in through the back door. The man bolted out the front entrance. The policemen tackled him and quickly subdued him. Hussey announced, "You're Hugh Lynn, and you're wanted for the murder of Jack Green and Tom Taylor on Savary Island."

Lynn replied, "It's too bad, I was expecting someone to come for me. I'll have to make the best of it."

Jenny was taken into custody as a material witness. The officers found Louis in Tacoma, where he went to school. Jenny said she had sent him there to keep him safe from Lynn.

Hugh Lynn had been captured on American soil, and according to the law, he should have been held in an American jail while Canadian authorities applied for extradition. In order to avoid that time consuming process, Jack Bledsoe bribed the skipper of the boat that took the party off Squaw Island. For ten dollars, the skipper made a slight detour into Canadian waters. There, Lynn was officially placed under arrest. The maneuver wasn't exactly legal, but in the nineteenth century such short-cuts were not uncommon.

Lynn was locked up in Victoria's Hillside jail to await trial. He claimed innocence, saying that Green and Taylor were alive when he had left Savary Island. He said he had known nothing of the killings until he heard the news from some Natives. He also allegedly said, "I'll shoot that damned Bledsoe if I die for it!"

In the meantime, Bledsoe, Hussey, and Anderson took Jenny back to Savary Island for another search of the crime scene. They found a pipe bearing the initials H.L. Then Jenny took them to a place near Comox where she, Lynn, and Louis had camped after the murder. The policemen found a bag of shot, a pair of pants identified as Lynn's, and the mast and sail of the abandoned skiff that had been found at Oyster Bay.

Hugh Lynn's five-day trial in Vancouver began on July 17, 1894, before Mr. Justice Montague William Tyrwhitt-Drake, Q.C. Defence Counselor Edward Pearce Davis faced the formidable Crown Prosecution team of Albert Norton Richards and Deputy Attorney General Arthur Gordon

Smith. Davis argued that his client had acted in self-defence. He allowed Lynn to take the stand and tell the story in his own words.

Lynn testified that he and John Green had been acquainted for a long time. On October 23, 1893, he arrived at Savary Island with Jenny and Louis. Green had offered him and Jenny winter jobs, which they'd accepted. He, Green, and Taylor spent most of the next day drinking, first over in Lund, and then back at the trading post. By the time they fell asleep that night, they had consumed a lot of whiskey.

The next morning, Lynn said, Green and Taylor got into a quarrel over who should light a fire in the stove and cook breakfast. Lynn said that he tried to calm them down, but the argument became more heated. In his rage, Green suddenly grabbed a rifle and shot Taylor dead. Then, to Lynn's horror, Green pointed the gun at him.

Lynn claimed that Green fired two shots at him, missing both times. Then the bolt on the rifle got stuck. Lynn seized the chance to rush at Green and wrestle the gun away from him. He ran outside with the rifle in his hands.

"I was out about five minutes," Lynn said. "He was standing up. I thought it would be all right and he would not get another gun."

But, according to Lynn, Green did get his hands on another gun, and he went after Lynn. Green was standing in the doorway with the weapon raised to fire, when Lynn saw him. "I fired and killed him," Lynn said. "I was confident he was dead. His feet stuck out past the door. I stayed outside for about half an hour before I went into the room." Lynn said that he fled because he was afraid he would be charged with murder. He admitted that he had put the shotguns in the dead men's hands, and had shot up the interior of the cabin and broken a window to confuse the police. But Lynn insisted that he had not murdered Green and Taylor.

Jenny hadn't witnessed the shooting. She testified that when Lynn returned from his trip to Lund to get more whiskey, he had given her a bottle. She sat in the guest cabin, and drank until she passed out. The next morning Lynn awakened her with a kick, and said they had to go — quickly! She said he was "acting crazy-like."

Jenny said that Lynn was wearing a new suit that morning, and his pockets were stuffed with plug tobacco. He also had three guns and a bag of bird shot that leaked pellets because it wasn't tied properly. Lynn put these into the skiff, along with some deer and mink pelts and a bear hide. Later, when they were camped, Jenny said that she saw Lynn count out $110 in bills and silver coins.

Lynn tossed two of the stolen guns into the sea. But he traded a .44 rifle to a man named Perego on San Juan Island, Washington, for another rifle. He sold the animal skins to a storekeeper named C.H. Smaley in West Sound on Orcas Island, Washington.

Prior to the trial, police had investigated Jenny's story. Perego and Smaley were in the courtroom. Among the objects the Crown presented as evidence were the .44 rifle, the bag of birdshot, and the stolen pelts.

A gunsmith testified that the samples of birdshot from Savary Island, the campsite, and the skiff were identical. He also said that the bullets found in the cabin walls and the bodies of the murdered men had probably been fired by the .44 rifle that the Crown believed was the murder weapon. Ballistic science was still a thing of the future, but the testimony of a firearms expert nonetheless carried a lot of weight.

Jenny testified that Lynn had often bragged to her about the murders. She said he had threatened her and Louis with a knife, promising to kill them if they ever breathed a word about the crime. Louis's testimony supported his mother's, to a degree.

The boy claimed that he had been spying on the men in the cabin, and saw Lynn kill Green and Taylor, then ransack the cabin. Davis objected to the seven year old's testimony as lacking in credibility. Justice Tyrwhitt-Drake overruled the objection and allowed Louis to continue. But when Davis cross-examined Louis, he got the boy so thoroughly confused that his testimony was dismissed.

Crown Prosecutor Richards cross-examined Lynn on his self-defence story for three grueling hours. According to a *Colonist* reporter, Lynn "stuck to his story with marvelous exactness under the circumstances." However, the evidence all pointed to Lynn as the killer. The fact that he had robbed the dead men before fleeing to the United States didn't support his claim of self-defence.

The jury deliberated for three hours, and then returned a guilty verdict with a recommendation for mercy. Davis immediately argued that such a verdict was not legally acceptable. At that time, a murder conviction automatically carried the death sentence, and it was up to the federal government to decide if clemency should be shown. Davis's point was that if the members of the jury did not think that Lynn deserved to hang, they should return a verdict of not guilty.

Tyrwhitt-Drake explained to Davis that the verdict as submitted by the jury was actually legal and acceptable. However, with no prompting from the judge, the foreman of the jury suddenly changed the verdict to an unconditional "Guilty!" Tyrwhitt-Drake sentenced Lynn to be hanged on August 24, 1893. The judge urged the condemned man to "spend whatever time is left to you in interceding with the throne on high for that mercy which you did not show these two unfortunate men ... The recommendation for mercy will be forwarded to the proper authorities."

The reason behind the jury's reluctance to send Lynn to the gallows was his obviously limited intelligence. And even though the jury had found Lynn guilty, some people thought that the evidence was almost entirely circumstantial. They also wondered how credible a witness Jenny really was.

A memorandum was sent to the prime minister, Sir John Sparrow Thompson, who was also minister of justice. The document did not dispute Lynn's version of what had happened on Savary Island. It noted, "The only other evidence as to the circumstances of the shooting is that of the klootchman [Native wife] Jennie [sic] Que-Ah-Boketo ... There is also some evidence that the deceased was quarrelsome when in liquor."

The decision as to whether or not Hugh Lynn's death sentence should be commuted to life imprisonment lay with Prime Minister Thompson. He considered the matter for four days. Then he sent his reply: "I think the report should be that the law should take its course."

The night before his execution, Lynn told William Moresby, the warden of the New Westminster jail, "I deserve all that I am going to get, and a great deal more." Lynn had a final visit from his mother, who had sat through the trial and wept when she heard the death sentence. He stayed up until after midnight, praying with two Presbyterian clergymen. Lynn awoke at 4:30 on the morning of August 24, dressed, and had a breakfast of steak, fried eggs, fried potatoes, toast, and coffee. Then he smoked a cigar.

At eight o'clock, he was taken to the wooden gallows that had been constructed in the jail yard. The executioner was probably a local man, because he had gone to great lengths to conceal his identity. He wore an oversized coat and hip waders. His face was hidden by a sack with eyeholes cut into it, and he wore a stained felt hat.

If Lynn was unnerved at the sight of the hangman, he managed to keep his composure. He asked the warden if he could exchange his boots for slippers. He had probably heard stories about hanged men who had

Library and Archives Canada PA-025798

Prime Minister Sir John Sparrow David Thompson, who was also Minister of Justice, decided not to commute Hugh Lynn's death sentence to life imprisonment.

kicked their boots off as they jerked at the end of the rope. Moresby granted his request.

On the scaffold, Lynn thanked the warden and the guards for their kindness. Then the hangman pulled the black hood over his head and put the noose around his neck. The knot was uncomfortable and Lynn, whose hands were tied in front of him, reached up and pushed it back. The clergyman on the scaffold had not completed the first sentence of the Lord's Prayer, when the hangman sprang the trap.

A reporter for the *Colonist* wrote, "the bolt was drawn and Lynn was swung into eternity. The neck was broken by the fall and death was instantaneous … after hanging for 35 minutes the body was lowered into the coffin under the gallows and later was removed for burial."

With Lynn's execution, the Savary Island murder case was officially closed. But a mystery still remained concerning John Green's money. There were rumours that he'd kept over $10,000 in his strongbox. Jenny testified that she had watched Lynn count out $110. Other people who encountered Lynn after the murders and before his arrest said he had as much as $600 on him. Green had purchased some real estate not long before his death, so it's possible that his money box didn't contain as much cash as people thought. Nonetheless, a legend grew that Lynn had stashed the bulk of $10,000 in loot on Savary Island. Treasure hunters have looked for it, but no one has found it. If slow-witted Hughie Lynn actually did have the presence of mind to hide stolen money, it was one thing he managed to do well.

# 7.

# THE LACROIX MURDERS:
## ROUGH NIGHT FOR THE HANGMAN

Canada's first official hangman was John Robert Radclive, an Englishman who had learned his trade as an apprentice to William Marwood, England's legendary virtuoso of the rope. Radclive was philosophical about his grim calling. In the absence of an expert executioner like himself, Radclive would point out, the job of hanging a convicted murderer would fall to a county sheriff who usually did not want the task. More often than not, county sheriffs were amateur hangmen who botched executions.

When Radclive would enter a death cell on the day of an execution to meet the condemned prisoner for the first (and only) time, he would tell the doomed man, "I am sorry for you, but I am but the instrument of the state. If it were not me, it would be someone else." Then he would softly say, "Come with me." The condemned man would often express relief that he was in the hands of a professional hangman, and not a nervous sheriff who didn't know how to carry out a quick, painless execution.

But even though he considered himself an angel of mercy, to condemned murderers at least, Radclive was aware of the feeling of revulsion the public has always had for executioners. Even in a time and place in which capital punishment was accepted as justice, the man who did the dirty work was a pariah. For that reason it was best if he entered town quietly, did the job, and then left like a phantom. On one assignment Radclive did not do that.

---

Stanislas Lacroix and his wife were not a happy couple. Lacroix was jealous beyond all reason. He suspected his wife of being unfaithful to him, and believed every bit of gossip about her that reached his ears. On one occasion, Lacroix thought that his wife was having an affair with his brother. In a jealous rage, he tried to cut his own throat. Lacroix's jealousy made him the object of jokes in Montebello, Quebec, where he lived with his wife and baby son. His neighbours' ridicule drove Lacroix to even greater fits of rage, making life unbearable for his long-suffering wife. By the summer of 1899, Madame Lacroix could endure no more. She left him. She fled to Montreal, then Hull, and finally found a home for herself and her child in Papineauville, a small town on the Ottawa River, a few miles upstream from Montebello.

For a year, Lacroix brooded, cursing his estranged wife and the people in Montebello, whom he held responsible for his unhappiness. He'd often get drunk at the local hotel, and say, of any neighbour whom he felt had wronged him, "He will pass (die) by my hand yet." Lacroix told the hotel keeper, Nelson Chenier, that his wife "would not die by any other hand than his." When Chenier warned Lacroix that he would hang if he killed his wife, Lacroix replied that it would not trouble him to mount the scaffold.

People who knew Lacroix were aware that he was capable of violence. He beat up one man who had angered him, and stabbed another man, though not fatally. But everyone dismissed the threats against Mme. Lacroix's life as drunken bravado. They did not realize that Lacroix was carrying a smoldering rage, which needed only a spark to ignite it into full flame. That spark burst in the summer of 1900.

In mid-August of that year, Mme. Lacroix returned to Montebello to visit friends. She was staying at the home of her friend Mrs. Commando at the western end of the community. When Lacroix learned that his wife was in town, he tried to arrange a meeting with her in the hope of patching things up. She refused to see him.

Lacroix was filled with a murderous rage, but kept it hidden. He borrowed a small amount of money from an acquaintance on the pretext that he was taking a trip to the United States. But when Lacroix had the cash in hand, he did not go to the train station. Instead, on the morning of August 24, he went to the Owen Brothers' store and bought a self-cocking revolver and a box of cartridges for $2.75. Joseph Robert, the clerk who sold him the gun, later testified that Lacroix "did not appear excited at the time."

That afternoon, fortified by liquid courage, Lacroix went to the house where his wife was staying and burst in. Sitting in the front room were Mme. Lacroix, holding her child on her lap, two or three of her female friends, and an elderly neighbour named Hypolyte Thomas de Trenchmontague. When Mme. Lacroix saw her enraged husband with a gun in his hand, she ran into the next room, clutching the boy. With the startled witnesses looking on, Lacroix followed her. He found her cowering behind a door, and dragged her out by the hair. She was still clinging to the child.

Mme. Lacroix managed to get to her feet and made a dash for the front door. Lacroix shot at her and hit her in the hand. She kept running. Lacroix followed and fired again. The bullet struck her in the neck, and she fell to her knees. Lacroix dragged his victim to the street. With the little boy still in her arms, the terrified woman cried, "Stanislas, what do you mean?"

In reply, Lacroix shot her through the heart. The murderer then went back into the house and gunned down de Trenchmontague, killing him on the spot. In his blind fury, Lacroix believed the old man had cuckolded him.

Leaving his wife dead in the street with her arms still around the child — who was miraculously unharmed — Lacroix fled town. A posse of armed men tracked him down to his brother-in-law's farm. Lacroix kept the manhunters at bay for several hours, threatening to shoot anyone who came near. He finally gave up and surrendered to a priest.

The shocking double murder made headlines across the country. In his cell in the Hull jail, Lacroix told a reporter from the *Montreal Star*, "I am doomed to die, and I'll have to see this out. All that you can do is pray for me. My action is a warning to young men not to drink, be jealous or listen to gossip. All that the gossip said about my wife was told to me and that made me mad."

Lacroix's case didn't go to trial until December of 1901, because his lawyer argued that he was insane at the time of the killings. However, doctors who examined the prisoner declared him sane and fit to stand trial. Lacroix's defence was that he had been driven to madness by his wife's infidelity; he claimed he did not even remember shooting de Trenchmontague. On Christmas Eve, a jury found Lacroix guilty of murder, and Justice Curran sentenced him to hang. Lacroix defiantly told the judge, "Fire your shot. I am ready. Radclive will never lay his hands on me. I am man enough to kill myself."

For a while Lacroix refused to eat, attempting to starve himself to death, but he gave up after a few days. He complained that the trial had not been fair, because his wife's infidelity had not been given proper consideration. He hoped that the federal government would review the matter and commute the death sentence. But Ottawa would not grant him clemency. The execution would take place, as scheduled, on March 21, 1902.

When Lacroix fully understood that he had no hope, he resigned himself to his fate and sought comfort in his Catholic faith. He spent his last days in prayer, and told his priest that liquor was the cause of all his troubles. Meanwhile, as the execution date drew near, an atmosphere of morbid anticipation fell over Hull. This would be the community's first hanging.

As expected, Radclive was given the task of dispatching Stanislas Lacroix. The executioner arrived in Hull a day early and took a room in the Windsor Hotel. Word quickly spread that the mysterious hangman was in town, and a crowd of more than a hundred curious men gathered outside the hotel. They were surprised to hear what sounded like a celebration coming from Radclive's window.

Instead of spending an appropriately quiet night on the eve of an execution, Radclive had picked up a few "friends," and was getting drunk with them in his room. The men gathered below became incensed at the sounds of "ribald songs and jests" that spilled out of the window. Some of them said that they heard Radclive boast about hanging Lacroix.

Nobody in the crowd doubted Lacroix's guilt, and to a man they would have agreed that he deserved to hang. That the official executioner was behaving as though he were on a holiday did not sit well with them.

Executions were occasions for solemnity, not drunken merry-making. Some of the men shouted threats against Radclive.

Radclive should have sent his guests home, turned off the light, and gone to bed. Instead, at about eleven o'clock, reeking of whiskey, he went downstairs to confront the ugly mob. He quickly got into a shouting match with a man who insulted him with foul names. Then Radclive allegedly said that he had come to Hull to hang a Frenchman, and he hoped it would not be his last.

Whether or not Radclive actually made such a foolish boast to a pre-dominantly French crowd, his behaviour certainly antagonized the mob. A man punched him in the face and sent him sprawling in the muddy street. Before he could get up, the crowd closed in on him. Angry men began kicking Radclive in the head. It seemed that everybody wanted a chance to stomp the hangman.

A police constable came to Radclive's rescue. He pulled the battered hangman out from under the flailing feet of the mob, and took him to the Cottage Hotel. Radclive's face was badly cut and bruised, and the Hull police decided that it would be a good idea to get him out of town. They quickly transported him across the river to Ottawa.

Radclive was taken under heavy guard to an Ottawa pharmacy for treatment. While his wounds were being attended to, a large crowd gathered outside. Anticipating trouble, the Ottawa Police Department sent a squad of constables and a patrol wagon to the pharmacy. The police decided that since the execution was taking place in Hull, Radclive was Hull's problem. They put him in a cab and sent him back across the river.

Radclive could not return to his hotel, so he went to the Hull jail. The sheriff put him to bed in a cell and locked the door, "in order that he may be in shape for his disagreeable duty tomorrow." The hangman was out cold for the night, but the sheriff feared more trouble before the hanging in the morning. He beefed up security at the jail, bringing in six Quebec Provincial Police officers and sixteen Dominion Police constables from Ottawa.

While Radclive was sleeping off the effects of the whiskey and the beating, Stanislas Lacroix spent his last, restless night in a cell just thirty feet away. Unable to sleep, he sat up praying with visiting nuns. He had not eaten any supper, and on his final morning he refused his breakfast. At 6:45 a.m. a priest arrived to say mass. Lacroix's three brothers and two sisters attended, and his own son served as acolyte. At the conclusion of the service Lacroix wept. He told his son to obey his relatives, lead an industrious and God-fearing life, control his temper, and never touch alcohol. He asked the boy not to feel unkindly toward his father, but to take a lesson from his terrible fate. Lacroix also appealed to his son to remember his mother affectionately.

A few minutes before eight o'clock the sheriff opened the door of Radclive's cell. The hangman walked down the hall to face Lacroix for the first time. "I am sorry for you," he said.

Lacroix held out his hand. "We might as well shake," he said, smiling faintly. "Do your work well. I am ready to die."

Lacroix's hands were bound in front of him so he could hold a rosary. He bore himself well as he walked out to the jail yard and climbed the steps to the gallows. On the scaffold with him were the sheriff, two priests, and Radclive. A crowd of about a hundred witnesses with special invitations were inside the jail yard. However, outside the walls over a thousand people jammed the streets. Spectators watched

Library and Archives Canada C-014078

Stanislas Lacroix on the gallows in Hull, Quebec. Radclive, the hangman, stands behind him. Note the people watching from nearby buildings and telephone poles.

from the upper storey windows of neighbouring buildings; some even climbed telephone poles for a good view.

Lacroix spoke in a strong voice as he said his rosary with a priest; Radclive had to warn the priest about standing on the trap door. When the prayers were finished, the priest told Lacroix to be brave and trust in God. Lacroix replied, "Je n'ai pas peur." (I am not afraid).

One of the priests addressed the crowd. He said, "Stanislas Lacroix will not speak. He authorizes me to say that he pardons all who have offended him, and he begs pardon of all to whom he has caused grief. He thanks everyone who has given him proofs of sympathy. He accepts with resignation the execution to which he has been condemned, and gives his soul to God in penance for his crime. He asks everyone to pray for him."

Radclive pinioned Lacroix's arms and legs, pulled the black hood over his head, and put the noose around his neck. At 8:05 he pressed the button that sprang the trap door. Lacroix dropped, but this time the execution was not carried out with Radclive's usual efficiency. Lacroix's neck did not break, and it took him thirteen long minutes to strangle to death.

The people who could see over the wall told the rest of the crowd that the execution had not been quick and clean. Authorities, afraid that there might be a repeat of the previous night's trouble, provided Radclive with a police escort across the river to Ottawa. Once there, he boarded a train for Toronto. Before his departure, Radclive told a reporter that he didn't think hanging did as much to prevent crime as some people thought. Then he added that he believed it was "a good thing — in some cases."

# 8.

# THE ATKINSON MURDER:
## LET THE DAMN FOOL HANG!

In 1913, Sydney, the largest city on Cape Breton Island, Nova Scotia, was booming. The Dominion Iron and Steel Company employed 2,500 men in one of the most important steel mills in Canada. Another 6,000 laboured in the collieries in nearby towns like Sydney Mines, Florence, and Glace Bay, keeping a steady stream of coal flowing to the coke ovens. Lured by the promise of a prosperous future, businessmen, speculators, and entrepreneurs flocked to Sydney. They invested in real estate, opened hotels and restaurants, and operated the great variety of shops and services the families of the miners and steelworkers needed.

Sydney's nineteen-man police department had little in the way of serious crime to contend with, but the constables were kept busy dealing with public drunkenness and common assault. The Nova Scotia Temperance Act was in effect, and the Sydney police laid 233 charges for breaches of that law that year. One of those fined in 1913 for the illegal sale of alcohol was a man named Ben Atkinson. Indeed, Atkinson was a repeat offender, having been caught in violation of the Temperance Act several times in the preceding two years. But it wasn't his bootlegging activities that got Ben Atkinson's name in newspapers across Canada. It was, rather, because he became the victim in a murder that shocked the tough town of Sydney.

Ben Atkinson, fifty-three, was a popular man in Sydney. Originally from New Brunswick, he was owner of the Minto Hotel on Charlotte Street. Atkinson was well-known among the harness racing crowd, and was even an accomplished driver. But the fact that the Minto Hotel was raided several times for violations of the temperance law suggests that Atkinson owed at least some of his popularity to the sale of illegal booze. Nonetheless, many respectable people thought that a bootlegger shouldn't be allowed to sing in the church choir, belong to a social club, or have membership in the Knights of Columbus or the Free Masons. All of which Atkinson did.

Ben Atkinson had married well. His wife Christina, known to family and friends as Tena, was a Maddin. The Maddins were a prominent family in Sydney. William Sr., the patriarch, had prospered as a contractor. His eldest son, William Jr., was deputy inspector of mines for Nova Scotia from 1882 until 1898, and was chief inspector of mines for the Yukon Territory in 1898. William Jr.'s son Jim studied law, and gained the reputation of being one of the best defence lawyers in Nova Scotia. Jim Maddin went into politics and was a Member of Parliament from 1908 to 1911. Prime Minister Robert Borden called Maddin one of the most promising politicians of the time.

Tena Atkinson was an extraordinary person in her own right. Unlike most other women of that period, she became involved in business. She assisted her husband in running the hotel, and invested in mine speculation and mineral rights. Tena's success in the male-dominated world of finance may have contributed to her unpopularity with other women in Sydney society. They considered her arrogant. Tena's response was disdain.

Tena had money, social status, and was well-travelled, having been all over North America. She had a daughter, Pearl, on whom she doted. However, by that summer of 1913, Tena evidently believed that the love had gone out of her marriage. She and Atkinson might even have been sleeping in separate rooms in the hotel. Tena certainly preferred the company of her brother William to that of her husband. In fact, William was often her travelling companion. They had just returned from a trip that had taken them all the way to San Francisco. Tena was also quite fond of William's son, her nephew Jim — the lawyer. He would play a significant role in the drama about to unfold.

On August 15, 1913, William Maddin and Tena Atkinson were camping on the shore of Front Lake, near Sydney. Like many of Sydney's affluent residents, they liked to get out of the city during the summer to escape the smell of the coke ovens and enjoy the beautiful Cape Breton countryside. With them was a business associate of William's, Dr. Kendall. Ben Atkinson had stayed in town to run the hotel, but would

*No. 94-1385-25880, Beaton Institute, Cape Breton University*

James Maddin, ca. 1910, Tena Atkinson's nephew and Frank Haynes' lawyer.

take short trips out to the camp. Ordinarily the Maddins and Atkinsons went to Sydney River, but William and Dr. Kendall wanted to investigate some potential investment property on Front Lake. They had been at the campsite for about two weeks.

At about six o'clock that evening, Atkinson arrived at the campsite with his daughter Pearl and her friend Greta Dixon. They were in an open buggy drawn by a grey horse. Tena went to the nearby McQueen family farm to cook some bacon and eggs, while Atkinson talked with Maddin and Kendall. After eating his supper, Atkinson climbed into the buggy for the drive back to Sydney. He had been in the camp for no more than an hour. The last time the people in the camp saw Atkinson alive, he was in his buggy heading down the Front Lake Road toward town.

After Atkinson's departure, William Maddin strolled over to the farmhouse and sat on the porch, enjoying a little casual conversation with John McQueen. As dusk set in, the men saw a party of young people approach on the Front Lake Road: Dougald, Kitty, and Peter McKeigan, along with Neil and Margaret McSween. They were on their way to a dance. Then young Duncan McQueen came into view, leading a grey horse and buggy. He had found them driverless on the road. He asked the McKeigans and McSweens if they had seen anyone on the road, and they replied that they had not. Duncan took the horse and buggy up to the farmhouse.

Everyone immediately recognized the horse and rig as Atkinson's. Concerned that he might have had an accident, William Maddin and John McQueen climbed into a wagon and dashed off to look for him. They hadn't gone very far when they found Atkinson lying dead on the road.

Another group of youngsters heading for the dance came along. Maddin told them to take his horse and wagon and hurry to Sydney to get Dr. John McDonald. By the time Dr. McDonald drove out to the scene in his automobile, the time was 9:50 p.m. Dr. McDonald brought along Dr. R.R. Bethune. Since there was an incline on the road where they stopped their car, Dr. McDonald placed a large stone under one wheel to keep the vehicle from rolling downhill. Later he would not be able to recall if that stone had been close to Atkinson.

The doctors quickly determined that Atkinson was indeed dead. His skull had been fractured. A closer examination in a mortuary the next day would reveal several wounds in the head, all of them clean and free of sand and gravel (which was not consistent with injuries from a fall). The right eye was discoloured, and one leg showed some bruising. Nonetheless, Dr. McDonald concluded that Atkinson's horse had caused Atkinson to be thrown from the buggy to his death on the road.

A wake was held in the Minto Hotel, followed by a service in St. George's Church. Then, William Maddin and Tena took the coffin by train to Atkinson's hometown of St. Stephen, New Brunswick, for burial. There was no proper autopsy, as the police saw no reason to suspect foul play.

One man, however, suspected that Atkinson's death had not been accidental. George Bryant, an old friend, thought it peculiar that the young people walking along the Front Lake Road had passed the very spot where minutes later the body was found, but had not seen a thing. The sun hadn't yet gone down, so Atkinson should have been clearly visible on the road. How could they not have seen him … unless the body wasn't on the road when they passed by! Moreover, Atkinson was a very good driver: it didn't seem plausible that he would be pitched from his buggy.

Taking far more initiative than the police, Bryant searched the "accident" site himself. Bryant would have made a good detective, for off in the bushes he found Atkinson's buggy whip and hat. Surely, the horse hadn't tossed them there! Then he discovered bloodstains in two locations off the road. Finally, still searching the bush, Bryant found a bloodstained, jagged rock that could have caused the injuries to Atkinson's head. He saw no rocks on the road that were large enough to crack open a falling man's head — aside from the one Dr. McDonald had put under the wheel of his car. But no one could remember just where that rock had been before the doctor moved it. Bryant's findings were enough to spur the police to examine the site themselves. They picked up a few more objects of interest.

After examining the evidence on the ground and witness reports from people who had been at the scene that fatal evening, the police deduced what had happened. Atkinson had been attacked on the road by a person (or persons) unknown, and killed. When the murderer heard people approaching, he took the body into the bush and hid until the coast was clear. The body was then dumped on the road and made to look like an accident victim.

The question of motive arose immediately. Atkinson still had $535 in his pockets — more than a coal miner's annual wages in 1913 — so it seemed unlikely that robbers had committed the crime. No one in Atkinson's family or wide circle of friends knew him to have any enemies. Some speculated that Atkinson had heard something in the woods, investigated, and was killed to keep him silent.

Among the objects the police found in the bush was a set of false teeth. Nobody, not even Tena, could say whether or not the dentures were Atkinson's. There were also some used matches, a couple of empty sardine cans, and two pages torn from *The Popular Magazine*. The name R.C. Goodwin was just barely legible on one of the magazine pages. The Sydney police discovered that an R.C. Goodwin had been staying at the Minto Hotel. They soon dismissed him as a suspect, but were interested to learn that a man named Frank Haynes had been a guest at the Minto at the same time as Goodwin. Moreover, there was some history between Atkinson and Haynes.

Haynes, thirty-eight, who sometimes went by the alias Frank Aubrey, was an American who was well-liked in Sydney, even though he was often broke and had to borrow money. He claimed to be an educated man with an interest in mining and minerals, but seemed to be something of a drifter. The Sydney police would eventually learn that Haynes was wanted in Arizona for bigamy, fraud, embezzlement, and forgery. One sheriff in that state called Haynes "the smoothest character ever to enter Arizona."

Apparently, Haynes was originally from Iowa, and his wanderings had taken him to the Klondike gold fields, California, and Winnipeg. He might have been involved in some questionable real-estate deals in Moose Jaw, Saskatchewan. He arrived in Sydney in July 1913, and took a room in the Minto Hotel. Ben Atkinson soon complained to the police that Haynes had tried to break into his private quarters. No charges were laid, but Haynes left the Minto and moved into a boardinghouse run by Mrs. Addie Stephenson.

The Sydney police began looking for Frank Haynes on Wednesday, August 27, but could find no trace of him in the city. Haynes had taken the ferry to North Sydney that very day and checked into the Belmont Hotel as F. Haynes of Chicago. The change of address had been rather abrupt, and Haynes had nothing with him but a valise and an umbrella. Staff at the Belmont would later say he seemed nervous.

The following morning Haynes returned to Sydney to have a sore tooth treated. Deputy Chief McCormick spotted him on Charlotte Street, and immediately told a constable to arrest him. Haynes blanched and said, "My God!" as the officer did his duty.

Once he was lodged in a cramped cell in the Sydney jail, Haynes regained his composure. He smoked cigars and read the books that were brought by his many friends. When a reporter asked how he felt, Haynes replied, "Oh, finely. Why should I feel otherwise? Were I anything but innocent, then there might be cause for worry."

The news that Ben Atkinson might have been murdered had electrified Sydney. Throughout the small city it was the main topic of conversation, from street corners in working class neighbourhoods to the parlours of the social elite. In spite of the fact that Frank Haynes was popular, there was a degree of relief in the community that the principal suspect was an outsider. There was also a considerable amount of criticism over the slipshod way the matter had been handled at the outset. Why, people wanted to know, had there been no autopsy? Why had there been no coroner's inquest? Why had it taken the efforts of a civilian, George Bryant, to prod the police into making an investigation? Moreover, by the time the police *did* search the grounds, a rainstorm had swept through and possibly obliterated other clues.

The preliminary hearing was held on Tuesday, September 2, 1913, before magistrate W.R. Hearn. The prosecutor was David A. Hearn (no relation). Haynes was defended by James Maddin, Tena Atkinson's nephew. By this time, Jim Maddin had gained the reputation of being almost invincible when it came to winning acquittals for men accused of murder. He was Cape Breton's own Cicero. But there would be questions about Haynes's wisdom in putting his fate in the hands of counsel so closely connected to the victim.

Duncan McQueen testified that he had been on his way home from milking the cows when he found the horse and empty buggy on the road.

They were some distance away from the place where the body was found. The young people who had met McQueen on the road all stated they had passed that place and seen nothing, and that it was still light enough that something as large as a man's body would have been clearly visible. Oddly, William Maddin said that by that time it was actually quite dark, and the youngsters could have walked past the body without seeing it. The Maddin family still held that Atkinson had died in an accident, and was not a victim of murder at all. The first mention of Frank Haynes came when a witness said he had seen Haynes washing his face in a brook near the McQueen farm a week before Atkinson's death.

Other witnesses not only stated that they had seen Haynes in that vicinity, but also that he had asked questions about the Atkinsons. Mrs. McQueen said he even stopped at the house and asked if she took in boarders. Meanwhile, a Sydney dentist identified the dentures found near the murder scene as a set he had made for Ben Atkinson.

Addie Stephenson said that Haynes had been boarding at her house and was there most evenings. But he had not been in his room the nights of August 16 and 17. She said that she did not know where he had been.

Charles White was a Sydney jeweller who had befriended Haynes and loaned him money. Haynes had told him he was expecting funds from Winnipeg. White testified that Haynes spent the night of August 15 at his house. White said Haynes showed up early in the evening complaining of a toothache. White gave him something for the pain, and then Haynes went to bed. Later, White checked on his guest before retiring himself, and saw Haynes fast asleep. The following morning, August 16, White loaned Haynes three dollars because he said he'd had nothing to eat for two days.

White said he was certain of the date, because on the 15th a woman named Annie Fowler had been in his shop to purchase a broach. If Miss Fowler could confirm that date, Frank Haynes would have a solid alibi as to his whereabouts on the night of Atkinson's death, and his absence from Addie Stephenson's house the following nights wouldn't matter.

The court located Annie Fowler, and at first she said she had indeed purchased a broach from White on August 15. Then she said she had made a mistake; she had actually bought the broach on a later day. Frank

Haynes had no alibi! Charles White unwittingly hurt his friend's case when he admitted that Haynes had repaid seven dollars of the debt he owed, and said he would soon pay the balance. Where did Haynes get that money?

A witness named Calvin Steeves testified that on several occasions following Atkinson's death, he had driven Haynes out to the Front Lake Road, and had waited in the buggy while Haynes searched the bushes. Haynes never told him what he was looking for. Finally, one day Haynes emerged from the woods with what Steeves said was a package about two feet long. The Crown later said the package contained a gun with which Haynes had intended to shoot Atkinson if the blow to the head didn't kill him. As a result of his testimony, Steeves was charged as an accessory after the fact.

As the preliminary hearing continued into the second week of September, people filled the courtroom and crowded the downtown area every day. They fought to gain admittance, like children squabbling over first place in a movie theatre line-up. One day the crowd was so unruly, the proceedings were delayed for half an hour while officers settled things down. Every new development in the case became grist for the rumour mill.

William Maddin gave the gossip mongers plenty to talk about when he admitted that Frank Haynes was known to the Maddin family prior to his arrival in Sydney. William had met Haynes in Winnipeg in April or May, and had discussed mining matters with him. William also said he had never seen Haynes in the vicinity of the McQueen farm.

Then on September 9, Tena was called to the stand. She stunned the audience when she testified that she had met Frank Haynes even before her brother had! Tena told the court she became acquainted with Haynes in San Francisco in February. He offered to sell her stock in a property called the Lucky Boy mine. The two met again in Marshfield, Oregon, where Pearl Atkinson attended school and William Maddin had an office. According to Tena, William (whose testimony had said nothing about meeting Haynes in the United States) allowed Haynes and a partner the use of the premises to show Tena some samples from the Lucky Boy mine. Haynes offered her what appeared to be a very generous deal.

But Tena didn't gain a reputation for being a shrewd business woman for nothing. She had made inquiries, and was warned that the Lucky Boy was not a good investment. She turned down Haynes' offer. But they must have parted on friendly terms, because a few weeks later they met again in Winnipeg. It seems this was not a chance encounter. Tena said she knew that Haynes was going to Sydney, and that they had even discussed doing some business promotions once he arrived there.

When Haynes was staying at the Minto Hotel, Tena said, he had a room right across the hall from hers. He wasn't there long before trouble began.

"I don't know why he left the hotel," Tena testified. "There was some talk of locks being tampered with. I told him he was suspected. He flew into a rage and asked me if I thought he was guilty of such a thing. He then said he would leave the hotel. My husband told me not to have any business dealings with him."

Tena admitted that she saw Haynes three times after he left the Minto. Twice she met him on the street, and once he stopped into the hotel to see if he had mail. She said she did not see him at all after her husband's "accident."

The scandalous story of Mrs. Atkinson and the American rogue swept through Sydney. Nobody was willing to believe that the relationship between Tena and Frank Haynes was based strictly on business. After all, *his* room at the Minto was right across the hall from *hers*. And what *decent* woman had business meetings with a man without her husband present! Then Pearl testified that she saw her mother with Haynes in Winnipeg and again in the hotel in Sydney, adding another perspective to the tales of shameless behaviour.

On September 19, the preliminary hearing concluded. Magistrate Hearn ordered Frank Haynes to go before the Grand Jury in February for further inquiry into Ben Atkinson's death. Haynes took it calmly. He was confident of an acquittal, and the prospect of prolonging his stay in the Sydney jail did not seem to bother him. He told the press that he got along very well with the other prisoners, who enjoyed his stories of travel and adventure. He praised the jailer, Jim Karn, calling him "a prince of good fellows." It's quite likely that Haynes took a fair measure of hope from the fact that the Crown had failed to establish a reason for him to murder Atkinson. Without a motive, and with only circumstantial evidence, the prosecution would have difficulty gaining a conviction.

However, David Hearn was not idle as he awaited the trial date. He brought in a Halifax detective named Hanrahan to do some sleuthing for the Crown. The record of the evidence Hanrahan collected has been lost, but the details were compelling enough to bring about the arrest of Tena Atkinson and William Maddin on October 6. Tena and her brother were charged with complicity in the murder, with being accessories before the fact as well as accomplices. If found guilty, they could hang! The *Sydney Daily Post* reported, "The case now promises sensations little dreamed of when the investigation started."

Two weeks after their arrest, Tena and William appeared in court. David Hearn argued that William Maddin had attempted, in every possible way, to interfere with the investigation into Atkinson's death. Hearn said Maddin had meddled with witnesses and had lied at the preliminary hearing. Moreover, said Hearn, after Atkinson's murder, Maddin had given Calvin Steeves money to pass on to Haynes. Maddin admitted giving money to Steeves, but said it was payment for some work Steeves had done for him.

The charges against Maddin were dropped due to insufficient evidence. Those against Tena would also have been dismissed, but she wouldn't have it. She was well aware of the gossip and the innuendo, and she wanted a full investigation that would clear her name. At Tena's own request, her case was bound over, and she put up a bond in security of $7,500.

The arrests of Tena and Maddin must have caused Haynes to reconsider his situation, because he attempted to escape. During the daytime, Jim Karn allowed Haynes the freedom to roam the corridor outside his cell. Using a pair of iron hooks he had somehow obtained, Haynes started hacking at the concrete wall. He hid his work behind an old mattress. Haynes thought that if he could make a hole large enough to crawl through, one night he would get out of his cell and make a break for it. A Frenchman named John Bosfet, who had been arrested on a minor charge, was in the cell next to Haynes. Since Bosfet was due to be released soon, Haynes tried to talk him into helping him get out of the country. Bosfet pretended to go along with the scheme, but when he was released he told Karn everything. Karn found the marks on the wall behind the mattress, and confiscated the hooks. After that, Haynes had to spend his days in the narrow confines of his cell.

Tena Atkinson and Frank Haynes were brought to court on February 19, 1914. Presiding was Mr. Justice Drysdale, QC, a former attorney general of Nova Scotia. Prosecuting for the Crown once again was David Hearn, with the assistance of D.A. Cameron. Tena and Haynes were defended by James Maddin and A.D. Gunn, who in addition to being a lawyer was also the mayor of Sydney. The attention of the whole city was focused on this trial, and the courtroom filled up quickly. Once the seats in the spectator section were full, the police locked the doors.

The charge against Tena was conspiracy to commit murder. Drysdale said that he had gone through all of the evidence, and could find no proof that she had actually conspired with Haynes to murder her husband. He saw no reason to return a true bill against her, and recommended

No. 91-568-22529, Beaton Institue, Cape Breton University

The old Sydney Courthouse ca. 1912, where Frank Haynes went on trial for his life.

that she be dismissed. The Grand Jury agreed, and Tena was discharged. However, the judge believed that in Haynes's case there was definitely need for further investigation, and the Grand Jury quickly found a true bill against him and committed him for trial.

D.A. Cameron opened for the Crown by reviewing the evidence, which he admitted was circumstantial but nonetheless left no doubt that Atkinson had been murdered. He stated, "If Atkinson fell out of the wagon and sustained an injury from which he bled copiously, it is impossible to believe that he would have walked eighteen feet off the road and deposited false teeth in one place, and then laid down in two other different places leaving large blood stains."

As to the question of Frank Haynes's involvement, Cameron said the Crown would produce witnesses whose testimony would confirm that the accused had been stalking Ben Atkinson for weeks. Moreover, Cameron said, they had the testimony of Calvin Steeves, who had taken Haynes out to the Front Lake Road after the murder, to search for an object the Crown believed was a gun. In the course of the trial, Hearn and Cameron called on fifty-nine witnesses. Their evidence, though largely circumstantial, pointed to Haynes as the killer.

The most damning testimony was that of John Bosfet. The Frenchman said that when Haynes asked for his help with the jailbreak plan, he pretended to play along. Bosfet said that he told Haynes that he had a brother who kept a motor boat in Sydney Harbour. Haynes wanted Bosfet to bring the brother and the boat into the escape plot. The brother was to bring food, clothing, and a revolver. Bosfet claimed that Haynes said, "The next man try to catch me, I shoot him like a rabbit." Bosfet said Haynes also wanted him to get some morphine that he could put in Jim Karn's tea. Haynes allegedly told Bosfet he had $20,000, and asked Bosfet to go to South America with him.

So far, Bosfet's testimony had only described Haynes's plan to escape custody. What he said next — if it was true — almost amounted to a confession of guilt.

According to Bosfet, Haynes began to confide in him as they continued discussing the escape plan. He said that Haynes told him, "I am here just for fighting another man. I was walking on the road. The man came in a wagon. He told me to stop. I stopped and he came at me. I am a strong man and I put him down. He get up and he come at me again. I put him down and hit him in the head with a stone and left him there."

Bosfet said that no one had told him to feign friendship with Haynes or trick him into talking. Even so, the members of the jury might have taken his story with a grain of salt. But the evidence was there in the Sydney jail that Haynes had tried to escape. The prosecution marked that as an indication of guilt.

The case for the defence suffered another blow when Tena Atkinson took the stand. She had told the police and the preliminary court that she'd had no communication with Frank Haynes between the time she'd met him in Winnipeg and the day he signed in at the Minto Hotel. Now, because of evidence given by telephone operators, she had to admit that she had in fact had a long telephone conversation with Haynes. She had even met him in New Glasgow before he arrived in Sydney. Tena insisted they had talked about real estate, and nothing more.

A real estate agent named Jim Donalds testified that he had known Ben Atkinson well, because they shared a love of horse racing. Donalds said he often visited the Minto Hotel. He was aware that Atkinson frequently had large amounts of cash on him. Donalds said he was also acquainted with Frank Haynes, and had loaned him money on several occasions, usually so Haynes could buy food. He told the court that shortly before Haynes was arrested, he had paid back all the money he owed. Donalds mysteriously added, "I was never on the road where the body of Atkinson was found." Jim Donalds would come to figure quite dramatically in the Frank Haynes case.

Another witness was Alex Simpson, manager of the Sydney YMCA on Charlotte Street. He testified that Haynes often went to the YMCA to use the telephone. On one occasion, when Haynes was not there, Simpson took a call from a woman who wanted to speak to Haynes. When Simpson asked for her name, she refused to give it. Simpson told the court that a week after Atkinson's death, he had lunch with Haynes in a restaurant. The American had always been dead broke when he showed up at the YMCA, but at lunch that day he showed Simpson a wallet stuffed with cash. Simpson also said that on August 26, Haynes had asked him to go along on a buggy ride. They went out to Sydney River, where Haynes met Jim Donalds and talked to him for some time.

It was quite evident that Frank Haynes, penniless for much of the time he had been in Sydney, suddenly had money after Atkinson's death. This was perplexing to everyone following the case, because Atkinson had not been robbed. Or had he? Could it be possible that Haynes had killed Atkinson in the course of a hold-up, but had found only *some* of the victim's money?

Frank Haynes was certainly worried about having to explain his windfall. Shortly after his arrest, he had written a letter to a woman named Dolly Bownes in California. He wanted her to provide him with an explanation for the money. Haynes's letter also suggests that he had been in some trouble in Los Angeles.

My Dear Dolly

I'm in a whole lot of trouble, and was arrested on August 28th as a murder suspect in this place. I was never so surprised in all my life – and just because I was walking out several times in that part of the country. You know why I left L.A. and why I wanted to get as far away as possible. I had intended coming back on the 29th or leaving here on that date, and now this terrible charge was placed against me. Dolly, before my God, I did not have anything to do with this and as I am away from friends and no money — I'm locked up here in the county jail and the days are awfully long and you know, dear, how I worry. I am nearly crazy. You know, dear, we have been the best friends for twelve years and our meeting again in L.A. was sweet to me — and Dolly, I know you will do anything in your power for me, as far as you can, and I'm going to ask you one now and it lies wholly in your power to help me get out of this, and what I want you to do is this.

If anyone should write and ask you if you sent me any money say yes, you sent me $150 by letter and that I should have received it about 17th or 18th of August, and that you mailed it to me in bills and that you didn't register it; and if they ask you what kind of bills, $10 and $20 and that you sent it from Seattle and that it was Canadian money. I don't think they will ask you what kind of money, but be prepared to answer if they do.

The reason for all this is — they think this man was murdered and I was hired to do it. It is about killing me dear and if you can help me this much I can make my case pretty clear. Won't you do this much for me, dear, for God's sake help me this much. I am almost crazy with this jail. You know I would not harm a kitten and that I never spoke ill of anyone in my life, and as soon as you receive this please wire my attorneys here at this place. I have retained them in case and I believe they are the best there is, and as soon as you receive this send a night letter to them saying you have received a letter (they will write you too) and that it was all O.K. Please do this for me Dolly and you will help save me, and I have every confidence in you and know you will and that will be all there is to it. For I had nothing to do with this in the world, also you say, if you are asked, that I called you such pet names as Teen, or Patsy or Baby Doll, won't you? I will send you or have the attorneys send you a transcript of the evidence also the newspapers so you will know as soon as you receive a reply from them they will want to know where to address a letter when I write you again (?). Don't forget the wire. God bless you, dearie, for I am depending on you.

Yours anxiously
"Montaluo Fred"

This letter was presented in court by the prosecution, and was proven to be in Haynes's handwriting. It must have been taken to court in the original envelope, because the Sydney postmaster recognized it as one that James Maddin had sent as registered mail. Evidently, Dolly Bownes knew Frank Haynes well enough that she didn't want to get mixed up in his scheme, and turned the letter over to local authorities. It was even rumoured that she was actually an employee of a private detective agency. The letter was sent to David Hearn by the Los Angeles chief of police. Whatever the scrape was that had caused Haynes to leave Los Angeles in a hurry, the law in that community seemed willing to help its counterpart in Sydney convict him. James Maddin's objections to the letter being admitted as evidence were overruled.

Dan MacDonald, a Sydney postal clerk, testified about yet another potentially incriminating letter. He said that on August 25, Haynes had been at the post office and had talked about Atkinson's death, which Haynes called an accident. Then Haynes had given MacDonald a letter which the clerk said was addressed to Tena Atkinson. MacDonald was certain of the letter and the date. Tena flatly denied receiving such a letter.

James Maddin tried to attack the credibility of some of the Crown's witnesses, but without much success. When the time came for him to address the jury, he placed the greatest emphasis on the fact that the prosecution had still not established a motive.

"It has been the custom throughout," he said, "with the best English jurists that when a man is charged with a crime that the Crown not only allege that against him, but they allege why he did it. They must supply a motive. The Crown has not supplied a motive. Every action in a man's life is a result of a motive, from the time of the first murderer Cain, who slew his brother from jealousy and hatred."

Judge Drysdale's address to the jury lasted four hours. In it, he expressed considerable suspicion regarding Tena Atkinson, even though all charges against her had been dismissed.

"Some parts of Mrs. Atkinson's evidence are remarkable," he said. "She met Haynes at San Francisco, again at Marshfield and then at Winnipeg. By this time you are halfway across Canada. This is testimony that I cannot make out, and I do not think you can. She says she did not see Haynes again until she came to Sydney, and when faced by the telephone operators from New Glasgow, says she forgot about it in the preliminary examination ... Do you think Mrs. Atkinson told the truth when she said she forgot about New Glasgow? She never forgot it. She was screening him in regard to the day she was in New Glasgow. Then she comes home and finds him quartered in her house. On the very day she moved out to Mira, Haynes began to frequent that road. We find him there on the 6th, 7th, 10th, 11th, and 12th, and it is suggested that as soon as the woman moves, the man follows … this woman's evidence was most extraordinary and some parts of it I simply cannot believe. What it all meant, I cannot say. The jury will have to speculate on it."

The jury retired. Eight hours later they returned with a guilty verdict! Frank Haynes twisted a piece of paper in his hands, but otherwise demonstrated no emotion. Judge Drysdale adjourned court until the following morning.

That evening in Sydney's five movie theatres, the word *guilty* flashed on the screens. Audiences loudly applauded and shouted their approval. The next morning, February 26, 1914, Drysdale sentenced Frank Haynes to hang on Friday, May 8, 1914. Outside the courtroom, in front of a noisy crowd, Haynes calmly lit a cigarette and waved to a few people he knew. He had nothing more to say … yet!

Even though Haynes had been convicted, the question of his motive was still the number one topic of conversation in Sydney. If not robbery, could the murder have been a crime of passion? Was Haynes keeping quiet to protect Tena Atkinson? If that were indeed the case, was the condemned man willing to go to the gallows for her? If Haynes *did* make a confession that implicated Tena, it wouldn't help his cause, because such an admission would finally reveal a motive.

The nagging absence of a motive cast a shadow of doubt on the guilty verdict. James Maddin and A.D. Gunn decided to use this as grounds for an appeal to the Supreme Court of Nova Scotia in Halifax for a new trial. The appeal was denied, which meant the defence could not appeal to the Supreme Court of Canada. Maddin and Gunn therefore went to Ottawa to appeal to the federal Minister of Justice, Charles Doherty, for a retrial. This was an unusual course to take, but it was not unprecedented in Canadian legal history. This appeal was also rejected, so Maddin and Gunn went to work on having the death sentence commuted to life imprisonment. In this the counselors had at least a glimmer of hope. Of the 179 death sentences handed down to convicted murderers between 1900 and 1914, almost half had been commuted. In 1913 Canadian judges had sentenced twenty-three people to death, but only eight had actually gone to the gallows.

While Maddin and Gunn were pleading his case in Ottawa, Haynes was sweating it out in the Sydney jail. On Tuesday, May 5, word came that Ottawa had dismissed the appeal for a new trial. The execution would take place, as scheduled, on May 8. Haynes was not aware that his lawyers were still fighting to save his life.

On Thursday, May 7, the hangman arrived in Sydney. He was an American ex-patriot named Jack Holmes who had hanged twenty men in the United States before moving to Canada, where he had carried out six more executions. This was to be his first in Nova Scotia. The gallows was ready and waiting. But something had happened that should have altered the fate of Frank Haynes.

On the Wednesday, knowing only that his appeal had been rejected, Haynes sent for David Hearn. He asked the Crown prosecutor if there was any hope for him. Hearn said there was not. Haynes then asked for pen and paper so he could write a statement. Hearn told Haynes to just tell his story, and it would be put in writing later. Haynes's statement — of which no written record now exists, except second-hand newspaper accounts — was dramatic and would have far-reaching consequences.

Haynes said that from his first meeting with Tena Atkinson, he had been infatuated with her. In Sydney, he said, she told him that she wanted him to kill her husband. She would pay him $2,000 to do it. Haynes said that when he was in Tena's company, he felt confident that he could carry out the crime. But when he was away from her, he had doubts. Then he met Jim Donalds!

Donalds, the real estate agent who was Atkinson's friend, was broke. He told Haynes he would do anything to make some money. He agreed to help Haynes kill Atkinson.

On August 15, 1913, Haynes said, Tena telephoned him and told him Atkinson was visiting her summer camp that afternoon. She said Atkinson would be alone on the drive back to Sydney, and that would be a good opportunity to kill him. Haynes and Donalds lay in ambush in the brush beside the Front Lake Road, in a spot they had scouted out earlier. The two men had taken positions on either side of the road, with Donalds a short distance down from Haynes. When the unsuspecting Atkinson came along in his buggy, Haynes let him pass. Then, as the buggy reached Donalds's hiding place, Donalds jumped out and grabbed the horse's head. Before the startled Atkinson knew what was happening, Haynes ran up from behind, grabbed Atkinson by the throat, dragged him from the buggy, and hauled him into the woods. Donalds followed.

Haynes told Hearn that Donalds picked up a rock and smashed Atkinson on the head with it. Atkinson crumpled to the ground. Donalds went back to the road and turned the horse and buggy around so the rig was headed back toward the McQueen farm. This was a prearranged signal for Tena, to let her know the job had been done.

Meanwhile, Haynes said, he kicked Atkinson's prone body once or twice. He said he realized then that they "had gone too far, and that the job would have to be finished." Donalds returned and started to carry the body out to the road, but they heard the group of young people approach. The killers remained hidden until they passed. Then they dumped the body on the road, expecting that Atkinson would appear to have been the victim of an accident.

Haynes told Hearn that he and Donalds then hurried back to Sydney, each man taking a different route. Haynes said he stopped only to wash the blood from his hands in a stream. He and Donalds did not meet again for three or four days.

In the meantime, Tena had given Haynes $400 as partial payment. She told him to split the money with Donalds. Haynes said Donalds was supposed to receive $1,000 and he told Tena she had better pay Donalds the balance, or they could be in great danger.

Then Haynes said that he and Tena had made plans for the future. He was supposed to get out of Sydney and wait for her somewhere. As soon as Tena had cleared up her husband's estate, she would join him.

This "confession" was certainly perplexing for David Hearn. If Haynes had agreed to kill Atkinson so he and Tena could run off together, why would she be obliged to pay him $2,000 to do the job? What did

Frank Haynes expect to gain by making such a statement? Was he trying to shift the burden of guilt to Donalds, who in this version was the actual murderer? This would not have saved Haynes, who was still a willing accomplice. In fact, by making this confession, Haynes irrevocably sealed his own fate.

Hundreds of miles away, in Ottawa, James Maddin and A.D. Gunn were desperately trying to save Haynes's life. They had convinced Minister of Justice Dougherty to call a meeting of the cabinet to consider commuting the death sentence. Back in Sydney, Crown Prosecutor David Hearn, who for months had been doing his best to send Haynes to the gallows, now found himself in something of a paradox: he needed a stay of execution!

Haynes had clearly implicated Tena Atkinson and Jim Donalds in the murder. That called for further investigation. Moreover, it meant Frank Haynes would be needed as a witness. Jim Donalds was arrested and locked in the Sydney jail. Tena was placed under house arrest in the Minto Hotel. Wagging tongues said that she, too, should be behind bars, but the police thought that the Sydney jail was no place for a woman, especially when there was about to be a hanging. Still, there were rumours of "preferential treatment" from citizens who considered Tena the real villain in the tragedy, even though Haynes's story was still unproven and very suspect. There were whispers that Haynes had turned against Tena because he'd heard she was going to marry a North Sydney hotel owner named John Gannon. It was reported that when Tena was told Haynes had confessed, she said, "I'm glad the suspense is over; it was killing me." Then, when informed that she was being charged as an accessory after the fact, she said, "Oh my God!" and fainted.

In Ottawa the cabinet was meeting to discuss commutation. A.D. Gunn was in the corridor, awaiting the decision. Suddenly Doherty came out with a telegram in his hand. He told Gunn that the cabinet had been on the verge of commuting the death sentence, when the telegram arrived. It was Haynes's confession!

Gunn asked, "Has it implicated anyone?"

"Yes," Doherty replied. "Mrs. Atkinson."

"All right," Gunn said. "Let the damn fool hang."

Gunn went back to the hotel where James Maddin was waiting and told him about the confession.

"Is anyone implicated?" Maddin asked.

"Your aunt," Gunn replied.

Maddin said, "Let's go to a movie."

Maddin and Gunn had decided to throw Haynes to the wolves to protect Tena Atkinson. Maddin might very well have still been able to persuade the cabinet to commute the sentence, or at least get a stay of execution. He could certainly have argued that Haynes had made the confession to the Crown prosecutor without benefit of counsel, making the whole thing illegal. But in Cape Breton at that time, blood ties could be even more binding than the finer points of the law. Maddin was not going to fight for Haynes's life, only to see his Aunt Tena placed in jeopardy.

David Hearn, however, was now doing everything possible to have the execution postponed. There was an intense and rather convoluted debate in legal circles over whether or not Haynes's confession would be admissible in court. Hearn argued that it was. He said that to hang Frank Haynes on schedule would only protect Tena Atkinson and Jim Donalds from prosecution if they were guilty, or leave them forever in the shadow of suspicion if they were innocent. The matter of granting a stay of execution came down to Judge Drysdale. After much argument, he finally decided to let the execution proceed. "Haynes must hang," Drysdale said. "The law must take its course. I shall not lift a hand to stay the carrying out of the sentence."

At 5:30 on the afternoon of May 8, Frank Haynes was taken from his cell to the gallows. To the guard, Jim Karn, he said, "Goodbye, Jim. You have been kind to me." As Haynes stepped onto the trap door, he whispered something to the attending physician, Dr. Brookman. The doctor put a morphine pill into Haynes' mouth. Holmes the hangman pulled the black hood over the prisoner's head, and adjusted the noose. Then he sprang the trap and Haynes plunged to his death. Twenty minutes later the body was cut down. It was quietly buried in Sydney's Hardwood Hill Cemetery. The charges against Tena Atkinson and John Donalds were eventually dismissed since there was no evidence to support them.

A few months later Tena sold the Minto Hotel and moved to the United States. She eventually moved back to Sydney, where she died in 1953. She was buried next to her murdered husband in St. Stephen, New Brunswick.

James Maddin continued to have a stellar career as a criminal lawyer, and became a police magistrate in Sydney. Of the sixty people charged with murder whom he defended, only two were executed: Haynes and a Halifax man named Lou Bevis, who had killed a police officer. When Maddin was seventy-five a journalist wrote of him, "Jim Maddin has struck many a blow for Oliver while appearing in from 60 to 70 murder trials." People who knew Maddin well believed he could have gone far in politics. But the man who had once been considered a rising star by Sir Robert Borden may have been haunted for the rest of his life by the spectre of Frank Haynes.

James Maddin died in 1962, and was buried in Hardwood Hill Cemetery, not far from Frank Haynes's unmarked grave.

# 9.

# SINNISIAK AND ULUKSUK:
## THE MISSIONARY MURDERS

In the early part of the twentieth century, the federal government of the Dominion of Canada had jurisdiction over the vast Arctic land that few Canadians had ever actually seen. Much of the frozen wilderness was still an uncharted, inhospitable mystery. Its harsh lands and ice-locked waters had been probed by only a handful of explorers. A relatively small number of white trappers, traders, whalers, policemen, and missionaries had first-hand experience of the hazards of life in the Far North. Most of these adventurers held the typical patronizing attitudes toward the indigenous peoples of the North, who were then called Indians and Eskimos. To the whites, these Native peoples were savages who had to be taught the rules of Western civilization and Christianity. Missionaries proselytized among the Natives, thrusting a strange religion upon them. At the same time most of these whites made little or no attempt to understand the cultures of the people they were attempting to convert to the "right" way to live.

In July 1911, a veteran Arctic adventurer named John Hornby showed up in the outpost of Fort Norman on the Mackenzie River with some exciting news. The previous summer, while exploring the country north of Great Bear Lake, he had encountered a group of Inuit who had never had contact with white people. As far as Hornby could tell, these Eskimos were untouched by "civilization." They had come down from Coronation Gulf, about 241 kilometres to the northeast, following the migrating caribou. Hornby had learned that they arrived in that region every year at the end of August, then headed north again with the first snowfall. These people carefully tried to avoid any encounters with the Barren Land Indians, whom they feared. They had never heard the word *Canada*.

Word of Hornby's "discovery" reached Father Gabriel Breynat, a Roman Catholic missionary who was the bishop of all of northwestern Canada. For years Breynat had been ministering to the Dogrib, Hare, and Slave Lake Natives. He had been praying for an opportunity to teach the Eskimos of the Far North the Gospel of Christ. Breynat had written, "No one knows how many they are, or what they are like, but we would like to send a few specimens to Paradise."

Breynat's Catholic Mission of Saint-Therese had competition from the Anglican Mission of the Holy Trinity. As one Catholic missionary put it, "We have against us here, a silent, vexatious and persistent opposition on the part of a handful of Protestants, freemasons and materialists, old-fashioned adherents of Darwinian theories who think they are in the vanguard of progress." Breynat was afraid that these Protestants might get to the Eskimos with their heretical brand of Christianity before the Catholics, so he decided to send a man into the field immediately.

The missionary Breynat chose for the great task was thirty-year-old Father Jean-Baptiste Rouviere. A native of France, Father Rouviere had arrived in the Northwest Territories in 1907. He had spent four years working among the Natives, first at Fort Providence on Great Slave Lake, and then at Fort Good Hope on the Mackenzie River. He was a quiet, patient man who had dedicated himself to the difficult life of a missionary. During his years in the North, Rouviere had taught Natives to make the sign of the cross, baptized their children, gave catechism classes, and learned a little of their language. But he did not venture far from the frontier posts, and so had no real experience in fending for himself in the wilderness.

Nonetheless, Rouviere welcomed the opportunity to become an apostle to the Eskimos. He responded to Breynat's challenge with a quotation from Isaiah: *Ecce ego, mitte me* (Here I am, send me forth). Rouviere would be starting out as a lone missionary, but Breynat promised to send him an assistant at the first opportunity.

Father Jean-Baptiste Rouviere was mild-mannered and patient.

*Missionary Obletes, Grandin Archives, Alberta Provincial Archives OB.3509*

That same July, Rouviere set out on the difficult journey to the far side of Great Bear Lake. He was accompanied by John Hornby, whom he trusted even though he had never met the man before. On August 15, 1911 (Assumption Day on the Catholic Calendar, and therefore auspicious to the priest), near the Dismal Lakes, Rouviere met Inuit for the first time. It was a small group of hunters. He later wrote (in French) of the event.

> There's no doubt about it: these are Eskimo. Thanks, O mother Mary. One of the first points of my mission is about to be fulfilled. Be pleased to bless this first encounter. As soon as they see me they come towards me. One of them is walking in front, holding his arms to the sky and bowing at the same time. I reply by raising my arms aloft, and immediately they increase their pace. When they get close to me, the man who was walking in front turns to the others and calls to them the single word "Krablunar" — "It's a white man." He comes towards me, gives me his hand and takes me by the arm to present me to the whole group. I was wearing my cassock and carrying my Oblate cross. The latter strikes them at once. They look at it and I try by signs to tell how He who is on the cross was sacrificed for us.

Rouviere enthusiastically shook hands with each man. Then he hung crucifixes around all of their necks. The hunters no doubt thought the priest's behaviour strange, but they seemed to like him enough to invite him back to their camp for a meal. Rouviere ate with his new friends, and "struggled to make them understand that I had come on their account and to stay among them."

With Hornby's help, Rouviere built a small shelter on the shore of a lake that would one day be named after him. He was delighted when local people came to see him every day, and he wrote that he found them to be very friendly and generous. Rouviere was certain that he would soon be making converts. However, he was very frustrated in his efforts to learn their language. The priest also had absolutely no understanding of Inuit spiritual beliefs or of the great respect they had for their shamans. To missionaries like Rouviere, shamanism was either childish foolishness or outright devil worship. It also annoyed Rouviere that Hornby, who had no interest at all in missionary work, would go off for extended periods of time, leaving him alone in an alien environment, with people with whom he could barely communicate.

At the end of October the Inuit broke camp to move north to the ice, where they would hunt seals. Rouviere could not go with them. He had no choice but to go to the place on the Dease River where Hornby had a cabin. He hoped that after the winter he could return to the task of converting the Inuit.

Hornby was a skilled hunter and Rouviere learned how to ice fish, so the two were never short of food. George and Lionel Douglas, prospectors who were friends of Hornby, had a cabin a few miles away. The Douglas brothers would often visit, and the men enjoyed playing cards and chess. The tough frontiersmen liked the quiet, gentle-natured priest. The brothers later said that Rouviere "added greatly to the pleasure of our life in winter quarters."

In March 1912, Rouviere returned to Fort Norman to prepare for a new expedition among the Inuit. At the Ste. Therese Mission, he met the priest who had come to assist him. A few years younger than Rouviere, Father Guillaume Le Roux was also a native of France. He had been in the Canadian North for about a year.

Father Le Roux was allegedly from an aristocratic background. He was very well-educated, a student of philosophy, and reputed to be a gifted linguist. He had already picked up some of the local Native dialect, and it was expected that he would learn to speak "Eskimo."

But Le Roux had none of Rouviere's easy going, patient nature. He was aggressive and overbearing. He had a hair-trigger temper, and when contradicted he was known to fly into fits of rage. Even though Father Le Roux was a dedicated Roman Catholic priest, he wasn't happy with his assignment to accompany Father Rouviere to the Barren Grounds. He preferred the relative comfort of Fort Norman, and the company of his colleagues in the Ste. Therese Mission. When the Douglas brothers met Le

Roux, they thought him domineering and insolent. Moreover, it appeared to them that Father Le Roux considered himself, and not the older and more experienced Father Rouviere, to be the leader of the missionary team. John Hornby also took a quick dislike to Le Roux.

Father Guillaume Le Roux had an overbearing nature and a quick temper.

Missionary Oblates, Grandin Collection at the Provincial Archives of Alberta OB.2736

In mid-July, with the help of Native guides and porters, the two priests set out on a grueling, six-week journey to the lakeside hut Rouviere had used the previous year. It was to be their headquarters. While Rouviere worked to improve their living quarters and caught fish for food, Le Roux gave his attention to a camp of about sixty Inuit. He was pleased to see that they had learned to make the sign of the cross. But even though Le Roux had shown an aptitude for learning Native dialects, he had a very difficult time with the language spoken by the Inuit. He wrote to Bishop Breynat, "I was able, Monsignor, to note a few words, see a little into the language, but it was very little that I could gather this year.… It is a labour so slow that I can scarcely see if we are getting ahead."

Meanwhile, Rouviere wrote of his concern that Father Le Roux was showing signs of weariness. But that did not mean they were giving up. "We will eventually know enough of the language to tell the Eskimo that we are missionaries.… Some day they will know how to render true homage to God."

The priests showed the Inuit colourful pictures of heaven, and tried to explain to them that if they accepted Jesus Christ as their saviour, they would go to the "land above the skies" when they died. They sang hymns to the people and fed them pieces of bread in preparation for the day when the converts would be ready to receive Holy Communion. The Inuit in return gave the priests new names. Rouviere was called Kuleavik, and Le Roux was called Ilogoak.

At the end of October, the Inuit departed again for the north coast. The priests had tried, unsuccessfully, to convince a family to stay and spend the winter with them. For all the hospitality the Inuit had shown the missionaries, they still had not whole heartedly accepted them. Among other things, they knew that the white men associated with the Indians, whom the Inuit feared. The priests had to retreat back to the Douglas brothers' cabin on the Dease River. The brothers were away, but they had left the cabin well provisioned for the missionaries.

In January of 1913, with John Hornby as his guide, Father Rouviere went to Fort Norman. A month later he headed north again. In April, Father Le Roux returned to Fort Norman "to renew his strength." He stayed until July 17. When Le Roux bade his colleagues at the Ste. Therese

Mission *au revoir* that day, he was telling them goodbye for the last time. Neither Rouviere nor Le Roux would ever be seen again by anyone in the white community.

Throughout the summer of 1913, the priests in their isolated post sent letters to Bishop Breynat via Native hunters and trappers. In late autumn, Breynat received a letter from Le Roux which said that he and Rouviere had decided the time had come for them to follow the Inuit to the northern sea. There, Le Roux said, they could live with the Eskimos and learn their language and way of life. He felt that he and Rouviere had become familiar enough with the Far North and the people to succeed in their mission. He expected they would be gone for about two years.

Something else, however, had galvanized the priests into leaving their headquarters and striking out into the Arctic wastelands. They had learned from the Natives that a Church of England mission led by a Reverend Fry was moving in on what they considered their territory. The Fathers had to make good Catholics out of the Inuit before the Protestants could get to them.

For several months Bishop Breynat heard nothing about Rouviere and Le Roux. That was not surprising, since they had ventured out into one of the most remote regions in the world. Breynat was well aware, too, that news travelled very slowly in the Far North. When the period of silence extended into many months, Breynat still felt no cause for concern.

The bishop became worried, however, when eventually rumours began to filter into Fort Norman that Inuit had been seen wearing priest's cassocks. Then a report came from a New Zealand ethnologist named Diamond Jenness who was doing field work among the Inuit. An Inuit hunter had invited Jenness into his igloo and proudly showed him a store of treasures. Jenness's report stated, "There were two rifles, a Hollis double-barrelled fowling piece, a pipe, plug tobacco, and part of an American magazine; strangest of all, a Roman breviary and an illustrated French Scripture book."

Some of these items might have come into the hunter's possession by any number of routes. But it was extraordinary that he should have the breviary and scripture book. Then came the alarming story that some Dogrib Indians told the explorer D'Arcy Arden. In 1914 the Dogribs had been hunting in the Dease River area, and had come upon the cabin that had formerly been occupied by Rouviere and Le Roux. They were astonished to find that the cabin had been looted and vandalized. This was most unusual, in a country in which a man could leave a cabin full of food and furs unattended for months at a time, and know nothing would be missing when he returned.

A little farther along the trail the Dogribs encountered a family of Inuit. There was a quarrel, and one of the Dogrib men seized an Inuit woman and threw her down. As she fell, two items she had been concealing in her bosom spilled out. The Dogribs didn't know what they were, but they were eventually identified as a paten (the metal plate a Catholic priest uses when serving Holy Communion) and a pall (the cloth used to cover the chalice used in the mass) with a cross on it. The woman's husband was wearing a priest's cassock, which had been cut off at the knees. There was a knife-hole in the garment, right over the heart. The material around the hole was stained with blood.

Now fearing the worst, Bishop Breynat requested that the Royal Northwest Mounted Police investigate. The task seemed impossible. The investigators would have to cover a vast, inhospitable terrain, questioning people who, in all likelihood, would be reluctant to talk to white policemen. But bit by bit, over long, frustrating months, the story of what happened to the priests was pieced together.

When the Inuit camp to which Rouviere and Le Roux had been administering broke up in late October of 1913, the people divided into small bands. Smaller family groups were more sustainable over the harsh winter than a large community. The priests were travelling with a man named Kormik and his younger brother, Hupo. Their group included two young men named Uluksuk and Sinnisiak. Uluksuk was a shaman who could reportedly perform magic.

John Hornby once had an unpleasant confrontation with Sinnisiak. Hornby had caught him trying to steal one of his sealskin fishing lines. Sinnisiak became angry and threatened to kill him. Hornby was stunned, because Sinnisiak's behaviour was so uncharacteristic of the other Inuit people he had met. But Hupo would later say, "Sinnisiak is a bad man, everyone says so."

Sometime after the fishing-line incident, Hornby warned the priests that the Huskies (a term the whites and Indians used for the Inuit) might not be as friendly as they seemed. In fact, some of the Inuit coveted the white men's goods, especially rifles and ammunition, but otherwise held the whites in contempt because they were unable to survive in the Arctic without help.

The Inuit and their missionary guests travelled north across the Barren Lands to a location just northwest of Bloody Falls. That was the site where the English explorer Samuel Hearne witnessed the massacre of Inuit men, women, and children by his Chipewyan guides in 1771. Hearne was horrified by the slaughter, and the story became entrenched in local Inuit lore. Ironically, another act of violence was about to take place near this bloodied ground.

Kormik's group moved on to the Coppermine River and set up camp a few miles from its mouth. They were starting to consider the priests a liability. The white men were useless as hunters, but had to be fed. They had no women to mend their clothes, so the women of the band had to do that work for them. The priests couldn't even make a snow house. In an environment in which every person had to contribute to the survival of the group, the priests were a burden. And they were quite possibly beginning to suffer from a depression-induced madness associated with the dreariness of the season. The Inuit called it *perlerorneq*.

Food was running low: the sea ice was still too thin for seal hunting, the caribou were unusually scarce, and the fishing was poor. The people didn't even have fish to feed their dogs. Rouviere and Le Roux were living in Kormik's tent, and rarely venturing outside. Both were probably suffering from malnutrition.

One night, Kormik stole a rifle belonging to Le Roux, and hid it among his own possessions. He thought that it made perfect sense that the best hunting weapon in the camp should go to someone who could put it to practical use. When Le Roux realized the gun was missing, he ransacked the tent until he found it.

Kormik, who was outside, was told about this. Enraged, he burst into the tent and threw himself on Le Roux. The missionary fought back in a most un-priestly manner. An elderly man named Koeha intervened, and pulled Kormik off Le Roux. The old man was no match for the young hunter, but Kormik had to respect the authority of an elder.

Koeha told Kormik to remain in the tent while he took the priests outside. He told them that they were in danger. Koeha warned them that Kormik wanted their blood. He said that they had to return south to their own hut immediately. "Next year," the old man said, "you will come back in better company."

While Kormik fumed, Koeha harnessed four dogs to a sled. Then he departed with the priests, having agreed to accompany them for half a day. At some lonely spot by the Coppermine River, the old man told them, "I am your friend. I don't want anyone to do you harm." He shook their hands. Then he left the missionaries to find their own way back to their cabin.

Rouviere and Le Roux were in a desperate situation. They were miles from their cabin. They had little food for themselves, let alone for the sled dogs. They had Le Roux's rifle, but they had neither the skills nor the strength to hunt.

For three days the priests struggled through the snow and increasing cold. They couldn't even make a fire. They had covered barely ten miles when Sinnisiak and Uluksuk overtook them.

The two Inuit said that they were hunting. Le Roux told them that they would be paid if they helped the exhausted, starving dogs pull the sled. Sinnisiak and Uluksuk agreed, and for half a day they put their backs to it.

By late afternoon, it was already dusk. Sinnisiak and Uluksuk stopped and made a small snow house. They put caribou skins on the floor, and invited the priests in to sleep.

The next morning the men awoke to bitterly cold weather and strong winds. Blowing snow made the going very difficult. The two Inuit lost the trail south, and went off in search of it. When they returned, they told the priests that they could not find the way. They wanted to return to their camp. The white men, who by now were practically incapacitated by hunger and cold, would have to continue their journey alone.

Then Uluksuk discovered a cache that the priests had made, evidently out of fear that the Inuit would rob them. In it were some axes, traps, and deerskins. But what caught Uluksuk's attention was a bag of rifle cartridges. Since the arrival of guns on the Barren Grounds, ammunition was so precious, it had become a form of currency. Uluksuk called Sinnisiak to come and see what he had found.

Now the priests were worried that the Inuit would steal their bullets. Rouviere grabbed a rifle from the sled and passed it to Le Roux. In a fury, Le Roux ran toward the Inuit, brandishing the weapon and shouting. The hunters did not understand a word he said, but they shouted back.

As the confrontation heated up, Rouviere began throwing cartridges into the river. To the two Inuit this was madness! Sinnisiak asked Le Roux if he intended to kill them, and Le Roux said he did.

Le Roux forced Uluksuk and Sinnisiak into the sled's harness at gunpoint. In spite of the horrendous weather, the pair had to pull the sled. If they stopped, or if the sled got stuck, Le Roux would point the gun at them and order them on. If one of them spoke, Le Roux would put his hand over the man's mouth. The Inuit decided that they would have to kill the priests before the priests killed them.

Under the pretext of having to relieve himself, Sinnisiak took off his harness and walked to the back of the sled. Le Roux, who had put the rifle down on the sled, pushed Sinnisiak and told him to get back into the harness. To show the priest that he had to answer nature's call, Sinnisiak started to undo his belt. Then Le Roux understood, and turned away. Immediately, Sinnisiak pulled out his hunting knife and stabbed Le Roux in the back. The priest lunged for the rifle at the same time that Uluksuk, who had removed his harness, also grabbed for it. They struggled over it, while Sinnisiak held Rouviere back with his bloodied knife.

Le Roux struck Uluksuk several times with a stick. The Inuit drew his hunting knife and stabbed the priest several times. Father Le Roux finally sank to the ground, dead.

Terrified, Father Rouviere tried to run. He had gone about 100 yards before Sinnisiak fired at him with the rifle. The first bullet missed, but the second one hit its mark. The priest sat down, wounded and bleeding. Uluksuk ran up with his knife and stabbed Rouviere twice. The priest fell backwards into the snow. Sinnisiak finished him off with an axe blow to the head. Then he hacked at the priest's legs with the axe, almost severing one of them.

Uluksuk sliced open the priests' abdomens and cut off pieces of their livers, which he and Sinnisiak ate. They believed this was necessary as protection from the vengeful spirits of the dead men. Then they covered the bodies with snow. Sinnisiak and Uluksuk took Le Roux's rifle, as well as Rouviere's, which they found in the sled. They also took several boxes of cartridges. The next day, November 2, they returned to their camp and announced, "We have killed the white men." They gave Le Roux's rifle to Kormik.

A day later, Kormik and several others went to the scene of the killings. They evidently stripped the bodies and pillaged the sled of anything they thought to be of value. Months later, the Inuit would loot the priests' cabin. To them, this was not stealing. The priests were dead and had no more use for their belongings, which were therefore free for the taking. In the Barrens, nothing went to waste. Many of the items were dispersed through trade.

When the Royal North-West Mounted Police (RNWMP) were first informed that the priests *might* have been the victims of foul play, this story was generally unknown. The police had nothing to go on but hearsay. They had no actual proof that the missionaries were dead. At the outset, the Mounties could only regard Le Roux and Rouviere as "missing persons."

Solving the mystery of the vanished priests was very important to the federal government. It presented an opportunity for Ottawa to affirm its authority over the Far North. Indigenous peoples had to be made to understand that the ground upon which they lived was Canadian, and that they must abide by the laws of Canada.

For the Mounties, this was an excellent chance for them not only to establish their rule of law on the Barrens, but also to grab some glory. The newspapers were filled with stories about the heroic Canadian Expeditionary Force, battling in the trenches of France and Belgium. This Arctic mystery would help put the legendary police force back in the public eye. Canadians would see that the constables who had brought law and order to the West and the Yukon were still the agents of justice on Canada's last frontier.

The job of tracking down the priests — or their killers — fell to Charles Dearing LaNauze, an Irish-born Mountie, and the son of a Mountie. Tall and broad-shouldered, LaNauze was adventurous by nature. He had been posted to various locations in the West, and as far north as Great Slave Lake. In the spring of 1915, LaNauze was in Regina and about to take a leave of absence so that he could go and fight in the Great War. However, his superiors prevailed upon him to lead the investigation, and promoted him to the rank of inspector. Two constables, Corporals James E.F. Wright and D. Withers, were assigned to assist him. In Edmonton, they were outfitted for a tough expedition that was expected to take two or three years.

The Mounties travelled to Fort Norman by rail and steamboat. There, LaNauze interviewed everyone he possibly could about the priests: missionaries, trappers, and Natives. He had the good fortune to recruit an Inuit interpreter and guide named Ilavinik who had worked for the Canadian Arctic Expedition and spoke fairly good English. Ilavinik agreed to guide the white men on the condition that his wife, Mamayuk, and daughter, Nagosak, accompany them. The woman and the girl, he explained, would be needed for cooking and mending foot-wear and clothing. Also joining the expedition were the Reverend Father Frapsauce, a missionary who could speak some of the Native dialects, and D'arcy Arden, who was sworn in as a special constable.

The party embarked on July 23, and did not reach the old Douglas cabin on the Dease River until September 8, largely due to stormy weather. LaNauze decided to use the cabin as a base of operations. He and his men spent two weeks hunting to lay in a supply of meat. Then he took a quick preliminary patrol out to the priest's ruined hut, about 113 kilometres away. The little building was hauntingly empty, and offered not a single clue as to the whereabouts of the former occupants. LaNauze returned to his base to wait out the winter.

Meanwhile, unbeknownst to LaNauze, the investigation was under way on another front. On August 12, 1915, Corporal Wyndham Valentine Bruce, of the Herschel Island detachment of the RNWMP, sailed east along the coast in the Canadian Arctic Expedition's ship *Alaska*. He established a base of his own at Bernard Harbour on Coronation Gulf. Assisting him were Diamond Jenness and a zoolo-gist named Rudolph Martin Anderson. These men had been working in the area and had become familiar figures to the Inuit. In their company, Bruce was able to conduct his investigation without arousing any suspicions.

Corporal Bruce spent several months travelling among the Inuit villages. He slept in snow houses, ate Inuit food, and even participated in rituals held by the shamans. With the assistance of a naturalist named Frits Johanson, Bruce found an Inuit cache that contained many Inuit artifacts and items that had obviously been obtained through trade with white whalers. Amongst these items were a Catholic Bible lesson book, a small brass communion plaque, and a priest's cassock. Printed inside the collar in indelible ink was: PERE ROUVIERE. Local Inuit told Bruce that the cache belonged to a powerful shaman named Mayuk, whom they called Rich Man.

Six weeks later, at the end of October, Bruce was in a village on an island in Coronation Gulf. There he was introduced to a man named Kormik. This Inuit was very friendly, and he proudly showed Bruce some prized possessions. He had a Catholic book called *Psalterium Breviarii Romani*, two coloured pictures of Jesus and the Virgin Mary, some old notebooks with French and Inuit words in them, and some linen handkerchiefs initialed with the letter *H*. Kormik said he got the handkerchiefs from John Hornby. But when asked who had given him the other objects, he only said, "another white man."

Bruce asked Kormik if he had ever met Father Rouviere and Father Le Roux. Kormik replied that he had seen two white men who wore long black coats and had beards who were called Kuleavick and Ilogoak. "These men went away hunting caribou in the summer," he said, "and I did not see them after this."

Bruce was certain that Kormik was lying, especially when the hunter showed him another package of items. The long list Bruce entered in his report included two handkerchiefs initialed G.R., a crucifix, priest's vestments, a bloodstained altar cloth, and a prayer book. Without betraying his reasons for wanting these things, Bruce traded Kormik six boxes of cartridges for them.

Corporal Bruce learned that Rich Man was also in the village. He visited his tent and was invited in to share a meal. Inside, Bruce watched as his host hung two rosaries and a crucifix attached to a long, black, silken cord from a support. The Mountie said nothing.

Sometime later, Bruce asked if he could look at some of Rich Man's treasures. The Inuit cheerfully obliged, and even said he had two more caches of such items stashed away. He said a white man had given them to him. Bruce noted everything in his report, and then returned to the base at Bernard Harbour.

On November 15, 1915, Rich Man arrived at Bernard Harbour. He agreed to trade several items in his possession to Diamond Jenness for some boxes of ammunition. One item was a Latin breviary with the inscription, G. LE ROUX, OBLAT DE MARIE IMMACULE. When Bruce asked him about it, with Jenness interpreting, Rich Man spun a long story about how these things had come to him through trade.

Corporal Bruce knew that Inspector LaNauze was headquartered on the Dease River to the south. In late January 1916, he led an expedition to try to hook up with LaNauze, but was forced to turn back by incredibly bad weather. Two months later LaNauze, who had no idea that another Mountie was working on the case, packed up his gear and headed north with his party toward Coronation Gulf. Because of snow-blindness, accidents, and foul weather, the journey took a whole month.

LaNauze's party reached the coast late in April, and on May 1 the inspector met Inuit for the first time. A band of fifteen people cheerfully welcomed the strangers into their camp and offered them food. Through the interpreter, Ilavinik, they were able to tell the visitors that some other white men were camped a short distance from them.

Like Corporal Bruce, Inspector LaNauze had the good sense to treat the Inuit respectfully. He was warmed by their hospitality. Through Ilavinik he told them that "The Big White Chief that lives far to the south" had only recently heard about the people who lived on the ice. LaNauze said he had not come to trade with them or to tell them about the land above the skies, but only to visit them.

Accompanied by two Inuit guides, LaNauze set out to find the neighbouring white camp. He left Ilavinik instructions to find out anything he could about the missing priests, but he advised him to be modest in his questioning, and not to interrogate anyone directly. LaNauze did not want to arouse any suspicions about the true nature of his visit.

A few hours hike from the village brought Inspector LaNauze face-to-face with Corporal Bruce. LaNauze was surprised to learn that another policeman had been investigating. He was also impressed with the evidence Bruce had gathered, even though there was still no actual proof that the priests were dead.

The Mounties spent the next few days moving from village to village, talking to the people through Ilavinik. The Inuit soon began to suspect that these white men were not just "visiting." But some of them knew Ilavinik either personally or by reputation, and they trusted him. Finally, on May 8, LaNauze got his big break in a large Inuit camp at Cape Lambert. LaNauze and Ilavinik were in a snow house speaking to two hunters who said they knew something about a pair of white men. LaNauze later wrote in his report:

> I then sat back and let Ilavinik do the talking. I heard him question them closely and I could see him trembling. I saw that something was happening, but I never moved, and in about five minutes he turned to me and said, "I got him, the priests were killed by Husky, all right; these men very, very sorry." And indeed they appeared to be; they both covered their faces with their hands, and there was dead silence in the igloo.
>
> I told Ilavinik to go ahead while I went out for Corpl. Bruce and when we got back Ilavinik said, "Now you write down these two names, Uluksuk and Sinnisiak, you got that? Now I find out some more."

By this time several more men had entered the snow house. One of them was the elder, Koeha. He gave the policemen a long statement about what had happened to the priests in his camp, and what Uluksuk and Sinnisiak said they had done. The old man concluded his story by saying, "I look for a long time to tell someone, for someone to speak for me, and now I speak. The two men that killed the good white men do not belong to my people. [We] are very, very sorry."

Koeha's wife corroborated his story, and more of the Inuit in the snow house stepped forward to say what they had seen and heard. It was evident to the Mounties that even though more than two years had passed since the killings, the people were still horrified by it. "We have carried this in our heads a long time," Koeha said.

When LaNauze asked why no one had ever told anybody about the killings, the reply was that the people were afraid. When Sinnisiak had threatened John Hornby over the matter of the stolen fishing line, Hornby had allegedly told him that if an Inuit killed a white man, all the white men would come and kill many Inuit in revenge. Blood feuds were common among the Inuit, so Hornby's words were taken seriously.

LaNauze now had to track down the wanted men. This would involve some hard travelling, but the task would not be as daunting as it might seem to people in the more "civilized" parts of the country. In the sparsely populated Barren Lands, people tended to move seasonally from one well known hunting or fishing place to another. Someone, somewhere, would know where the "fugitives" could be found.

With Rich Man as guide, LaNauze tracked Sinnisiak to a village on the ice off Victoria Island. The hunter was repairing a bow when the Mountie first saw him.

"What do you want?" Sinnisiak asked.

When Sinnisiak was told that he had to go with the white men, he was extremely frightened. He said that if the white men killed him, his ghost would seek vengeance on them. LaNauze assured Sinnisiak that he would not be killed. Because Sinnisiak was not a member of their community, the other Inuit urged him to go with LaNauze and not make trouble.

Corporal Bruce went through the formality of placing Sinnisiak under arrest. LaNauze told the prisoner he could take his wife and property with him, hoping that would put him somewhat at ease. Among Sinnisiak's possessions was a rifle that was later identified as Father Rouviere's.

The police party arrived back at Bernard Harbour on the morning of May 16, 1915. Sinnisiak was kept under guard in the camp kitchen. The next morning at a formal hearing presided over by LaNauze, Sinnisiak told his story through Ilavinik. The Mounties were stunned: if Sinnisiak's statement was true, the suspects had acted in self-defence. But Bruce and LaNauze were policemen, not magistrates. They still had to bring in Uluksuk.

LaNauze had learned that Uluksuk was probably hunting near the mouth of the Coppermine River. On May 18 he left Corporal Bruce in charge of Sinnisiak, and set out with Constable Wight and a sixteen-year-old Inuit known as Patsy Klengenberg. Jenness had highly recommended the boy as an interpreter. Also, Patsy knew Uluksuk personally, and could identify him.

After a tough, five-day trek, they found an Inuit hunting camp near the mouth of the Coppermine. Patsy immediately recognized Uluksuk. The wanted man ran toward them with his hands raised high in the traditional sign of peace and friendship. He was shouting at them. LaNauze heard the words, "*Goanna! Goanna!*"

According to Patsy, Uluksuk said, "Thank you, white men. I am Uluksuk. I will do whatever you want. Are you going to kill me now? I am ready. I have carried this in my head a long time. I am glad you have come."

Uluksuk asked only for time for his wife to finish making him a new pair of boots. LaNauze granted the request. When Uluksuk told his version of the circumstances surrounding the killing of the priests, the story matched the one told by Sinnisiak in almost every detail.

LaNauze took his prisoners to the RNWMP post on Herschel Island where they spent a dreary winter while he waited for instructions. Sinnisiak and Uluksuk did menial chores without complaint, and developed a taste for white man's food. LaNauze finally received orders to take the accused men to Edmonton for trial. Joining them as interpreters and witnesses were Ilavinik, Patsy Klengenberg, and Koeha. They made the journey by steamboat and train, arriving in Edmonton on August 8, 1917.

The RNWMP certainly got the good publicity the senior brass had wanted. Stories about the war in Europe had to share front pages with accounts of the "Famous Trip of Red-Coated Guardians of the Law," as one headline announced. The ethnologist William Thompson, who had travelled with LaNauze's party, told a reporter, "No other force of police could have done it. Had they sent three American detectives after these men there would have been three graves up north."

The Inuit were housed in the Edmonton Mounted Police barracks. They found the summer heat almost unbearable, even though they were given light clothing and provided with electric fans. Sinnisiak and Uluksuk were confined to their quarters, but the others were taken on tours of the city. While they gazed in astonishment at automobiles, tall buildings, and more people than they had ever seen in one place, they were themselves the objects of much public curiosity. The city dwellers wanted to see these exotic northern people who, according to one local editor, "are governed by the same natural laws as the animals and to kill is not a crime." It was from these readers of such ill-informed and sensationalistic press that the jury of so-called peers would be selected. The Inuit were bewildered by the stories about a far off place in which white men were killing each other by the tens of thousands every day. Their language had no equivalent for the word *war*.

Group photo taken in Edmonton, August 1917. Back row L-R: Charles C. McCaul, Crown Council; Inspector C.O. "Denny" La Nauze; James E. Wallbridge, defence counsel; Corporal James E. Wight. Front Row L-R: Ilavinik, interpreter; Koeha, witness for the prosecution; Sinnisiak; Uluksuk; Patsy Klenkenberg, interpreter.

*Glenbow Archives NA-2939-2*

The trial began on the morning of August 14, 1917, with Chief Justice Horace Harvey presiding. The courtroom was filled to capacity. For the sake of spectacle, and in spite of the heat, Sinnisiak and Uluksuk were dressed in their native garb: fur-trimmed caribou skins. In contrast, their long hair had been cut short so that they would look "civilized." Beside each prisoner was a tub of ice water, in case he wanted to put his feet in and cool off.

Inspector LaNauze, Corporal Bruce, and Constable Wight were conspicuous in their dress uniforms. Sitting next to the Mounties were two Oblate priests. They looked sombre and officious in their full-length black cassocks, with large crucifixes hanging from their necks on silver chains. They were witnesses for the Crown, present to see that justice was done for their slain brothers. Six white men, all non-Catholics, made up the jury. On a table that held items to be presented as evidence were a rifle, a crucifix, a blood stained cassock, and part of a human jawbone. This grisly relic, picked up by an Inuit hunter who visited the scene of the crime, was all that had been left by the wolves and other scavengers.

The Crown had decided to try the accused men separately. Sinnisiak was placed in the dock first, to be tried only for the murder of Father Rouviere. In his long opening statement, the senior prosecutor for the Crown, Charles C. McCaul, K.C., said:

> These remote savages, really cannibals, the Eskimo of the Arctic regions, have got to be taught to recognize the authority of the British Crown, and that the authority of the Crown and of the Dominion of Canada, of which these countries are a part, extends to the furthermost limits of the frozen North. It is necessary that they should understand that they are under the Law, just in the same way as it was necessary to teach the Indians of the Indian Territories and the North West Territories that they were under the Law … The code of the savage, an eye for an eye, a tooth for a tooth, a life for a life, must be replaced among them by the code of civilization.

McCaul took the whole morning session to deliver his statement. He consistently referred to the "barbarous Eskimos" as a threat to white travellers in the North. He used maps to show the jury the vast domain over which the lawless savages were spread. He praised the efforts of Christian missionaries who, since the earliest colonial times, had gone among the heathen tribes to spread Christianity, many of them suffering martyrdom. When McCaul described the terrible last days of Fathers Rouviere and Le Roux, he was moved to tears by his own eloquence.

McCaul's vocabulary was beyond Patsy and Ilavinik's grasp. Their translations were garbled at best. Several times Sinnisiak dozed off, either from the heat or sheer boredom, and had to be prodded awake.

When McCaul finished speaking at last, James E. Wallbridge, K.C., the attorney for the defence, stood up and demanded a new jury. "I must take great exception to my learned friend's address to the jury," he said. "The address has been unfair, and calculated to prejudice the jury by reason of the inflammatory remarks of council and it seems to me it would be hardly right to proceed unless you empanel a new jury. He made remarks to the jury which I think were very, very unfair." The request was denied.

The trial lasted three days. The Crown based its case on the statement Sinnisiak had made to LaNauze through Ilavinik. McCaul argued that Sinnisiak plotted with Kormik to get Father Le Roux's rifle. He deliberately trailed the priests with the intention of doing them harm. The priests, McCaul said, were in such desperate straits that they were entirely justified in using force to make the Inuit pull their sled.

Wallbridge countered that the defendant's statement hardly qualified as admissible evidence, since he would not have understood the meaning of LaNauze's official warning, "whatever you say may be given in evidence against you," even when it was translated by Ilavinik. In fact, Wallbridge disputed the sense of the entire judicial proceeding to "primitive men, savage men of the stone age." He said the defendant had acted in self defence.

When the last witness had testified and all the evidence was in, Chief Justice Harvey gave his instructions to the jury. Oddly, he told the six men that if they should find the "poor, ignorant, benighted pagan" guilty, he would personally recommend that the death penalty would not be carried out. He was certain that his recommendation would be accepted by the Governor General of Canada. Nonetheless, Harvey made it clear that he expected a guilty verdict.

The jury deliberated for just over an hour. They returned a verdict of … *not guilty*! Everyone in the courtroom was astonished. The court clerk, thinking he had not heard correctly, asked the foreman of the jury to repeat the verdict. Nobody was more confused than Sinnisiak. When Patsy translated the verdict for him, Sinnisiak said, "It is not true. I did kill him."

James Wallbridge was delighted with the acquittal, but Charles McCaul was furious. He was scheduled to prosecute Uluksuk in a few days. He demanded a change of venue, on the grounds that public opinion in Edmonton had become unfairly sympathetic to the Inuit, and unduly inflamed against the murdered priests. He felt that the jurors had been influenced by anti-Roman Catholic sentiments. There was even an unsubstantiated rumour, he said, that the priests had been "monkeying with the Eskimo women."

McCaul got his wish, and the trial was moved to Calgary. This time both defendants were tried for the murder of Father Le Roux. The proceedings opened on the morning of August 22, and again the trial lasted three days. Instead of their caribou skins, Sinnisiak and Uluksuk wore denim jail uniforms. This time the jury returned a guilty verdict, with a strong recommendation for mercy.

Chief Justice Harvey pronounced the death sentence, as the law demanded. But he told the interpreter, "Tell them, Patsy, that they have been found guilty of killing the priests, which they should not have done … but tell them that the Great White Chief will not be too hard on them … because they did not know our ways, that they did not know what our laws are, he will not put them to death for the killing of these men this time. They must understand, though, that for the future they know now what our law is and if they kill any person again then they have to suffer the penalty."

The death sentence was commuted to life imprisonment in the jail at Fort Resolution on the shore of Great Slave Lake. Sinnisiak and Uluksuk spent two years in jail, and then worked for a while as guides for the RNWMP. They were officially released on May 15, 1919. In 1924 Uluksuk was shot dead by another Inuit in a quarrel over a dog. Sinnisiak's fate is uncertain, though it is believed he died before 1930, possibly from tuberculosis.

# 10.

# THE BOOHER MURDERS:
## THE MIND READER

In the 1920s the "science" of psychic phenomena became something of a rage in Canada, the United States, and Britain. Men and women who claimed to be mediums, mentalists, and spiritualists were a huge draw in theatres and community halls, in big cities and small towns. They astounded audiences with "powers" that enabled them to read minds, predict the future, and even communicate with the dead. Sir Arthur Conan Doyle, creator of Sherlock Holmes, was a firm believer in spiritualism. Master magician (and Doyle's one-time friend) Harry Houdini denounced the practitioners of the "mystic arts" as a pack of charlatans. He exposed many of them as frauds who deceived people with cheap parlour tricks.

Nonetheless, otherwise rational, intelligent people clung to the belief that a select few had mysterious mental powers beyond the understanding of modern science. These gifted ones could "see" what ordinary people could not see, and could supposedly solve crimes that baffled even the most skilled police detectives. One such mentalist played a significant role in a case of mass murder that shocked Canada.

On the morning of July 9, 1928, no one in the village of Mannville, Alberta, would have thought that their small community, 170 kilometres east of Edmonton, would soon draw the attention of both the Canadian and international press. Mannville was a typical prairie town; an agricultural centre with one constable, who usually had to deal with only petty offenses. But on a farm four miles north of the village a horrendous tragedy was about to occur.

The Booher family came to Alberta from Oklahoma in 1906, lured by the prospect of good, cheap farmland. They moved around the province, finally settling on property north of Mannville in 1924. Neighbours knew them as good, hardworking people. Henry Booher was fifty in the summer of 1928, and his wife Eunice was forty-four. They had four children: Fred, twenty-five, Vernon, twenty-two, Dorothy, nineteen, and Algertha, seventeen. Also living on the Booher farm were two hired men: a Polish youth named Wasyl (Bill) Rosak, and Gabriel Gromley.

Monday morning, July 9, Henry left the house early. He had acquired a piece of land ten kilometres to the north and wanted to make a new homestead on it. He had built a rough shelter there, and expected to be away for the rest of the week. Henry was in this shack when disaster swept down upon his family.

At about six o'clock in the evening, Dorothy and Algertha saddled up a pair of horses to ride into Mannville for basketball practice at the public school. Their ten-year-old neighbor, Lowrie Creighton, had just returned one of the saddles. As they rode off, the girls saw their mother returning to the house from the strawberry patch with a basin full of fruit. They also saw Vernon standing by the gate to the north pasture. A colt tried to follow the girls, and Vernon had to chase it back. Bill Rosak was working with Fred in the west field, while on the other side of the Mannville Road, Gabriel Gromley was working in the east field.

Vernon would later say that when he got back from chasing the colt, he saw that Bill Rusak had come in with the team. Vernon pumped water for the horses. Then Will Scott, the reeve of the municipality, stopped by to deliver a tax notice. Scott was driving a horse and buggy, and had met the Booher sisters on his way out of town. He would testify that he saw Vernon walking up and down beside the house, apparently tossing a stone in the air and catching it. Scott and Vernon discussed the family's tax bill.

While they were talking, Scott saw Bill Rosak leave the barn and walk toward the house. Vernon called out to Rosak, telling him to feed the pigs. Rosak apparently did not hear, so Vernon shouted more loudly. This time Rosak heard him, and went to follow his orders. Scott saw him at the granary door with a bucket in his hand. Then Scott continued on his way, having spent just a few minutes talking to Booher. Vernon would claim that after Scott's departure, he went out to the fields to bring in the cows. He was about a kilometre from the house when he heard five or six shots. He took no notice of them: gunfire out in the countryside was not unusual.

Just to the west of the Booher place was the Ross family farm. Robert Ross had been working in the field that afternoon, and at six o'clock decided to call it a day and head back to the house. On the way he saw Fred Booher clearing stones. Robert and Fred exchanged neighbourly greetings, then each headed toward his own home. Ross had not yet reached his farmyard when he heard the shots. He, too, paid them no attention.

Ross walked into the yard just as his daughter-in-law Maude returned from a shopping trip in Mannville. As they entered the house Maude looked at the kitchen clock: it was twenty to seven. Sometime between eight and 8:30 that evening, the Rosses heard two more shots. Half an hour after that, Vernon Booher burst into their kitchen and gasped, "Someone has shot Mother and Fred!"

Vernon told the shocked Mrs. Ross to phone the doctor and the police. He told her to call the Mannville telephone operator, and get someone to keep his sisters from leaving town. Then, after asking for someone to get his father, Vernon turned for the door. Robert Ross tried to hold Vernon, but the young man bolted out the door and ran across the field toward his house. He didn't know that his sisters were already home.

Just after nine o'clock, Dorothy and Algertha unsaddled their horses and put them in the corral. Dusk was falling as they walked up to the house, and clouds blocked the light of the setting sun. When Dorothy pushed open the screen door, the house was dark inside, but in the fading light she could see Fred lying on the floor on his back, with one shoulder against the open inner door. He still had his hat on. Algertha was right behind Dorothy.

At first they thought Fred had fallen and hurt himself. Dorothy crouched down to feel his pulse. Then she saw the bloody wound in the middle of his face. She stood up and whispered, "He's been shot!"

Once their eyes had adjusted to the darkness, the horrified girls looked around and were jolted by a second shock. In the dining room, just an arm's length away, their mother sat silent and motionless in a chair, her body slumped forward on the table. Their hearts hammering, Dorothy and Algertha inched their way into the dining room, keeping their backs against the wall. As they drew near their mother, they could see that she, too, was dead.

The terrified girls ran out the front door and across the field toward the Ross farm. They hadn't gone halfway when they saw Vernon walking toward them. There was no need for words. They could tell from the look on his face that he already knew their mother and brother were dead. The three began to walk back to the house.

Robert Ross, meanwhile, had phoned Charles Stephenson, who lived about ten kilometres away, and asked him to drive out to Henry Booher's new homestead and tell him what had happened. Then Ross called Dr. Joseph Heaslip, the local physician. Ross asked him to call Alberta Provincial Police Constable Frederick Olsen in Vermillion, about twenty-six kilometres away, and tell him there had been a shooting. Ross also called the Mannville operator about keeping Dorothy and Algertha from returning home, but was too late.

Meanwhile, Dr. Heaslip told his wife to call the police, grabbed his black bag, and jumped into his car. He took but a few minutes to drive to the Booher farm. He was surprised when no one met him in the yard. Dr. Heaslip knocked on the door of the darkened house, but nobody answered. Nor was there any response when he called out. Then Dr. Heaslip heard voices coming from a field. He drove out, and found Vernon, Dorothy, and Algertha coming from the direction of the Ross farm. The girls were clearly in shock, but Vernon seemed to be holding himself together. When the doctor asked what the trouble was, Vernon said, "They are all dead up there."

Dr. Heaslip drove the three back to the house. He told them to stay in the yard while he went inside. The girls did as they were told, but when the doctor cautiously opened the front door, Vernon was right behind him.

The first thing he saw was Eunice Booher sitting dead at the dining room table. Her arms were sprawled across the table top, and between them lay a shattered bowl of strawberries. Her body was bent forward, with her head drooped below the level of the table top.

Dr. Heaslip struck a match and looked at Eunice more closely. The top of her head had been blown off, and some of her brain lay on the floor between her feet. Shaken, the doctor gasped, "My God! This must be the work of some maniac." A quick examination of the body indicated that Eunice had been dead for about two hours. Vernon told Dr. Heaslip to look in the kitchen.

While Vernon held matches so the doctor could see, Heaslip examined Fred Booher's body. Fred had been shot in the mouth, the bullet exiting through the back of his head. Another bullet had struck him in the neck and smashed through his right shoulder blade. There was also a bullet hole in the rim of his hat. The doctor estimated that Fred had also been dead about two hours. He concluded that the killer had shot Eunice from behind, but Fred had to have been looking the murderer in the face when he was gunned down.

Dr. Heaslip had served in the Great War and was well-experienced with gunshot wounds, but the carnage he found in that farmhouse rattled him. The night of horror wasn't over. Vernon told him there was another body in the bunkhouse!

The bunkhouse was a tiny wooden structure mounted on a wagon bed and wheels so it could be moved about during harvest time. It had two bunks, one above the other, and a single door. Inside, Dr. Heaslip found Gabriel Gromley's body. The dead man was face down on the floor. He had been shot three times, in the chest, neck, and jaw. From the evidence of blood flow, Dr. Heaslip could tell that the third gunshot wound had been inflicted after the other two. He didn't think this man had been dead as long as the other victims.

Outside, Dr. Heaslip asked Vernon and his sisters if they had any idea who could have committed the murders. Vernon said that the day before, two Hungarian men had come to the farm looking for Gromley. They'd tried to make him leave with them. Fred had told the strangers to get off the property. They argued with Fred, and then left.

The doctor asked if anyone else was around the farm. Vernon replied that a young Pole named Bill Rosak worked for the family, but he didn't know where he was. Dr. Heaslip wondered aloud if Rosak could be the murderer. Dorothy immediately spoke up for Rosak, saying he was a harmless kid who couldn't possibly be responsible for the brutal slayings.

News of the tragedy had already begun to spread. Dr. Heaslip drove Vernon, Dorothy, and Algertha to the Ross house where two neighbouring farmers — armed with guns — had arrived. Dr. Heaslip made a phone call to ensure that Constable Olsen was on his way. Then he and Vernon borrowed a lamp, a rifle, and a shotgun from the Rosses. Vernon, the doctor, and the two neighbours headed back to the Booher farm in two cars.

Meanwhile, Charles Stephenson and a neighbour named Cain had driven out to Henry Booher's homestead, where they found Henry about to go to bed. Stephenson could tell Henry only that there had been a shooting at his home, and that Eunice and Fred had been hurt. Stephenson drove Booher to the farm, arriving after Dr. Heaslip had left with Vernon and the girls. Henry went into the house and saw the awful truth. He came out ashen faced, and told Stephenson and Cain that his wife and son had been shot dead.

Leaving Cain to watch the house, Stephenson and Henry drove toward the Ross farm. On the way they met Dr. Heaslip's group. Vernon told his father that the girls were with the Ross family and Dr. Heaslip had a theory that a maniac was on the loose. The men all drove back to the scene of the crime.

When they arrived at the gate they found more neighbours had gathered there — grim-faced men carrying guns. As they waited in the yard for Fred Olsen, Vernon once again noted that Bill Rosak was absent. Taking Vernon with him, Henry went looking. Within minutes they found Rosak.

The young Polish farm hand was lying on the floor of the barn, about ten feet from the rear wall. Dr. Heaslip examined his fourth body that terrible night. A bullet had smashed into Rosak's nose and straight through his head.

Constable Fred Olsen didn't arrive at the Booher farm until 11:15 p.m. He had been out of the office when the call came in, and received the news late. Olsen was a veteran police officer with eighteen years of experience, first with the North-West Mounted Police, then the Alberta Provincial Police. He knew how to conduct the initial stage of a murder investigation.

Olsen looked at the four bodies and concluded that a high powered rifle had been the murder weapon. He took statements from everyone present and then sent everybody home — except town constable Gordon Milligan and Holburn T. Taylor, editor of the *Mannville News*. He also told Vernon not to go anywhere.

Something about Vernon's behaviour struck Olsen as strange. He took Vernon into the house for a private talk. A lamp was burning, and Eunice Booher's almost headless corpse was in plain view. Olsen saw that Vernon's hands were clean, which was unusual for a farmer who had supposedly been working all day. When, in the midst of all this tragedy and excitement, had Vernon taken the time to wash his hands? Olsen also noted that Vernon did not seem to be upset at the sight of his mother's body.

"How are your nerves?" Olsen asked Vernon.

"It is alright," Vernon replied. "This does not bother me at all."

Olsen asked if there were any guns in the house. Vernon said the family owned a shotgun and a .22 calibre rifle, both of which were kept in a rear bedroom. Olsen found both guns hanging on pegs, right where Vernon said they would be. The weapons were dusty and had obviously not been used in a long time. The shotgun had a broken hammer. Neither gun could have caused the wounds in the victims' bodies. However, under further questioning Vernon told Olsen that sometimes the men in his family borrowed a .303 rifle from Mr. Ross or Mr. Stephenson for hunting or slaughtering beef.

The following morning, July 10, Constable Olsen began a thorough search of the Booher farm as soon as the sun was up. Gordon Miller, Holburn Taylor, and Vernon Booher were all there. Olsen started with the bunkhouse. Two thin beams of sunlight piercing the dark interior drew his attention to a pair of bullet holes in the wall above the upper bunk. In one of the holes Olsen found a piece of nickel jacket from a .303 rifle bullet. He carefully searched the ground around the bunkhouse, but found no shell casings. The gunman had evidently picked them up. Was that really the act of a deranged maniac?

Inside the cramped farmhouse, Olsen concluded that the killer must have stood behind Eunice and shot her from point blank range. The bullet that killed her had ploughed a groove across the kitchen table and penetrated the front door. At first Olsen could find no shell casings in the kitchen. Then, determining where the killer must have been standing when he shot Eunice, Olsen stood in the spot and looked around. He noticed an enamel dishpan full of water on the floor beside the stove. He put his hand in the water and came up with something the killer had overlooked; the casing of a .303 rifle shell!

Olsen stepped outside and showed the shell casing to Milligan and Taylor. Vernon had been hanging around the front gate. When he saw the two constables and the newspaperman talking, he hurried over to see what was going on. Olsen dropped the casing into his pocket and said nothing about it to Vernon. As the policeman continued his investigation he noted that while Vernon seemed to wander around the farmyard with no evident aim or intent, he seemed to stay close to the house and the other men, as though watching and listening.

Out in the horse barn, Olsen found something that Dr. Heaslip had missed during his hasty examination in the darkness. In addition to being shot in the head, Bill Rosak had also been shot in the abdomen. Olsen concluded that at least nine shots had been fired during the mass murder, but he had found only one shell casing.

That afternoon Detective Sergeant Frank Lesley from APP headquarters in Edmonton arrived in Mannville with two other officers. Olsen met them at the train station and reported his findings during the drive to the Booher farm. After examining the crime scene, Lesley arranged for a local undertaker to remove the bodies. Then he sat down at the kitchen table and asked for Vernon to be sent in.

Vernon told Lesley that he had spent most of the previous day repairing fences. He had eaten supper with his mother and sisters while Fred and the hired men were still working in the fields. He recalled Will Scott's visit, as well as telling Bill Rosak to feed the pigs. Vernon said he was about three-quarters of a mile away from the house, looking for the cows, when he heard six or seven shots. He thought nothing of the gunfire at the time, but when he returned to the house after driving the cows home, he found his mother and brother dead. Then, he said, he had run to the Ross farm for help.

Lesley noted that in this account, Vernon said nothing about finding Gabriel Gromley dead in the bunkhouse. Yet, when Vernon had returned with Dr. Heaslip the night before, he already knew that Gromley was dead. Like Constable Olsen, Detective Sergeant Lesley had the uncomfortable feeling that Vernon was not telling the whole truth. He asked the young man if the family had any problems.

Vernon mentioned the two Hungarian strangers who had come looking for Gromley and had quarreled with Fred. He said there had been no ill feelings among any of the family members. He'd even loaned Fred money to buy a piece of land.

Henry backed his son up on that. Henry said there had been no trouble in the family, and he could think of no one in the community who would wish any of them harm. As Vernon had done with Olsen, Henry showed Lesley the dust-covered .22-calibre rifle and the shotgun with the broken hammer. He also said they sometimes borrowed a .303 rifle from Mr. Stephenson or Mr. Ross. Henry showed Lesley a dusty .303 cartridge box that had been in his and Eunice's bedroom. There were only three or four shells in it. Then, in Vernon's room they found another box of .303 shells, and this one wasn't covered with dust!

Constable Olsen had already spoken to the Rosses about their rifle, and they could account for it the night of the murders, right up until Dr. Heaslip had taken it before he'd headed back to the Booher farm with Vernon. While Lesley questioned Vernon and Henry, Olsen went to Charles Stephenson's farm to speak to him about his .303. Stephenson said that he did indeed own a .303 Ross army rifle, which he kept on a rack above the kitchen door. But the gun wasn't there! The men searched the house thoroughly, but could not find the rifle.

Stephenson said he had no idea how long the gun had been missing. He had loaned it to Fred Booher the previous winter, but Fred had returned it. Stephenson hadn't used the rifle since then. Aside from his own family, Stephenson said, the only people who knew where the gun was kept were Fred and Vernon Booher. Later, Stephenson discovered that the box of .303 shells usually kept behind some canned goods on a shelf was also missing. He said the only people outside his own household who knew where the box of ammunition was kept were Fred and Vernon.

Police located the two Hungarians who had argued with Fred. The men were questioned, but had solid alibis for the time of the murders. Both men were released. That left only one logical suspect.

With little solid evidence to go on, Lesley took Vernon into custody as a material witness. He had him locked in the closest thing Mannville had to a jail — a small cell in the village firehall — where Constable Milligan could keep watch on him. Later, Vernon was moved to a cell at the APP headquarters in Edmonton.

Meanwhile, the police needed to find the murder weapon, which they were certain must be Charles Stephenson's missing Ross rifle. Without that, their chances at getting a conviction were almost nil. Constable Olsen spent several days searching the buildings and fields of the Booher farm. If Vernon was indeed the killer, the rifle had to be nearby. But Olsen could find no trace of it. He dragged the well, hoping to at least turn up the shell casings, but there was nothing.

On Sunday, July 15, about fifty local farmers spent their only day off helping Olsen scour the fields and underbrush. In spite of an inch-by-inch search, the men and boys found neither gun and nor shell casings. It was as though Stephenson's rifle had vanished into thin air.

On Tuesday, July 17, Vernon was taken back to Mannville for a coroner's inquest in the town's Orange Hall. By this time the horrific story had become headline news across Canada and had even received coverage in the United States. American tourists drove all the way up to the little Alberta community just to cruise past the infamous Booher farm. The Orange Hall had the capacity for 500 people, and it was packed for the inquest.

There were discrepancies between the testimonies about the times witnesses had heard shots. Robert Ross said he had spoken to Fred Booher just before six o'clock. He'd heard a shot soon after that; just enough time, Ross speculated, for Fred to have reached home. Algertha testified that she had heard a shot shortly after leaving the farm at six o'clock. Then she claimed to have heard a shot as late as nine o'clock, about the time she and her sister returned home. Vernon testified that he heard five or six shots between 7:20 and 7:30, when he was out looking for the cows.

When Henry Booher took the stand he looked every inch the haggard man whose world had fallen apart. He had gone to Edmonton to ride back with Vernon on the train. Vernon appeared confident and relaxed when answering the court's questions, but Henry was hesitant, and his answers were guarded. He reluctantly admitted that two months before the murders, Vernon and Fred had quarrelled. The argument became heated, and Henry had been obliged to intervene. Soon after, Vernon had driven to Calgary. There, Vernon said, he had wrecked his car in an accident and injured his right arm. The arm was in a cast when he returned home, and he'd been able to do only light chores until a short time before the murders.

The verdict of the coroner's jury was that the victims had died as the result of gunshots fired by "some person unknown." Nonetheless, at the conclusion of the inquest Frank Lesley formally charged Vernon Booher with four counts of murder. Strangely, the young man didn't seem particularly worried.

The preliminary hearing began the next day in the Orange Hall, with Magistrate P.G. Pilkie presiding. Detective Sergeant Frank Lesley acted as prosecutor. The Booher family was well-off financially, and Henry certainly could have afforded to hire J.I. Jones, Mannville's only lawyer, to defend Vernon. But to everyone's surprise, Vernon said he would be defending himself. Magistrate Pilkie officially advised Vernon that although this was but a preliminary hearing, any statements he made could be used against him in a future trial. Vernon accepted the warning and said that he wished to proceed anyhow.

The police case, as presented by Frank Lesley, was that shortly after his sisters had left for Mannville, Vernon entered the house and shot his unsuspecting mother from behind while she sat at the table. That was the gunshot Algertha heard just after leaving the property. Moments later, Fred Booher stepped inside the kitchen door. Fred went no further, because Vernon gunned him down and then shot at him again as he lay bleeding on the floor. This accounted for the shot Ross said he heard not long after Fred left him. It did not explain why Ross heard only one shot, when others had been fired at Fred.

According to Lesley's scenario, Eunice and Fred were already dead in the house when Will Scott showed up with the tax notice, and Bill Rosak came in from the fields. The implication was that Vernon had carried out the killings in a meticulous, cold-blooded manner. What sort of man could casually discuss taxes right after brutally murdering his mother and brother?

After Scott's departure, Vernon went into the barn and shot Rosak. A neighbour had testified that he'd heard gunfire from the direction of the Booher farm at 7:45 p.m. Those shots were likely the ones that killed the Polish boy. That left Gabriel Gromley as the last potential witness to be eliminated. Lesley believed Vernon killed him in the bunkhouse sometime between eight and eight-thirty. Those were the shots Robert Ross and his daughter-in-law had heard. Then Vernon ran to the Ross farmhouse with his tale about finding his mother and brother dead.

Lesley said the probable murder weapon was Charles Stephenson's missing .303 Ross rifle. He told the court that the Sunday morning before the murders, the Stephenson farm was deserted because the family had gone to church. Like everyone else in the community, they didn't lock their door. Vernon had a perfect opportunity to enter the house unseen and take the gun.

But had Vernon, in fact, been seen? Lesley had witnesses who testified they had seen Vernon that Sunday morning, riding his black mare along a trail that led from the Booher farm to the Stephenson place. Dorothy Booher admitted that Vernon had indeed ridden off on his horse that morning. But she said he had gone to see the Austins, a family who rented a farm from the Boohers, and whose place was in the opposite direction of the Stephenson farm.

Lesley's case rested on the slimmest of circumstantial evidence, and Vernon knew it. Dressed in his Sunday best, Vernon was the picture of a man confident of his innocence. He cross-examined witnesses carefully, and pointed out flaws in their testimonies that challenged Lesley's version of the events. Vernon's courtroom manner, which earned him the grudging respect of the police officers who were convinced of his guilt, also won the sympathy of many people in the Orange Hall. Everyone had been surprised when Henry Booher mentioned the argument between Vernon and Fred, and Lesley attempted to use that to establish a motive. He said Vernon hated Fred, and in his deranged mind felt it necessary to kill his mother and the farm hands in order to murder Fred and make it all look like the work of some maniac.

But Henry angrily denied that there had been animosity among his children. Fred and Vernon's quarrel had been the sort that young men, even brothers, have all the time. Henry insisted that Vernon had no reason to hate Fred. Why should he? Vernon had always been the favourite son!

Observers had to admit that Lesley's case was weak, to say the least. One argument with his brother hardly seemed motive enough for Vernon to kill four people, two of them his own flesh and blood. And if he *did* do it, where was the murder weapon? Nonetheless, Magistrate Pilkie told Vernon:

> While the evidence is largely circumstantial, and contains several discrepancies as to time, still suspicion is directed toward you, and I do not feel that I should take upon myself the responsibility of liberating you, and therefore I must commit you to stand trial on the information laid against you. I can only hope that you may be able to prove yourself innocent.

Throughout the hearing, a small, foreign-looking gentleman sat next to Holburn Taylor at the press table. He occasionally wrote in a notebook, but most of the time he stared intently at Vernon Booher, scarcely twenty feet away. Most of the people thought the stranger was a journalist covering the sensational murder case. Others suspected he was a doctor, brought in by the court to study Vernon. The latter group was partially correct. The man was Dr. Otto Maximillian Langsner, and the APP had employed him as a special investigator. Thanks to the fascination the press had with all things extraordinary, Dr. Langsner would soon be a household name in Canada.

According to the stories that would soon fill Canadian newspapers, Dr. Langsner was a thirty-five-year-old native of Austria. He came from a wealthy family, and was exceptionally well educated. Among other things, he had studied psychology. Langsner had become something of a celebrity because of his alleged abilities as a hypnotist and a mentalist — a mind reader!

Langsner had been traveling the world as a showman, astounding audiences with demonstrations of his hypnotic and psychic "powers." In Honolulu, Hawaii, he met Dr. Hans Gressner, another practitioner of the "psychic arts." Gressner soon expressed an interest in forming a partnership with Langsner, and using their combined talents to help police solve difficult cases. Little wonder that Gressner was impressed with Langsner: according to his resume, Langsner was one of the greatest psychic criminologists in the world.

Langsner told Gressner that he belonged to the School of Applied Psychology in Nancy, France. He said that he was an honourary member of many of the world's great police departments, including Scotland Yard. He claimed to have worked for police in Vienna, Chicago, New York, and Montreal. In 1921 he had used his special powers to help solve an anarchist bombing case in Bucharest, Romania. In 1926 he had allowed himself to be "captured" by Chinese pirates, and then used his phenomenal powers to escape. The information he passed on to Britain's Royal Navy brought about the arrest and execution of eighteen pirate leaders. In Vienna, Langsner had solved a baffling murder case with the assistance of Sir Arthur Conan Doyle. He and Doyle had accomplished it, Langsner said, through a combination of telepathy and thought analysis.

All this important work for the forces of law and order did not come without a price. Langsner said he had received many threatening letters because of work he had done for police. Indeed, criminals in Persia had almost succeeded in assassinating him with poison. Of course, Gressner and other people whom Langsner told of his accomplishments had only his word that it was all true. Because of the nature of his work, Langsner said, there was a lot that he could not disclose. He also would not allow his picture to be taken for newspapers, as that could compromise his work as a criminal investigator.

Travelling with Langsner was his young and exotically beautiful wife. She was known to the public only as Madame Langsner, and claimed to be German. The doctor was often reluctant to talk to the press, but Madame Langsner was usually willing to entertain reporters with stories about her husband's power.

Langsner and Gressner decided that North American police departments would be most in need of their talents, so they sailed to Vancouver. There, Langsner tried unsuccessfully to obtain a recommendation from Dr. James G. McKay, president of the British Columbia Medical Association. Even though they were of some small assistance to the British Columbia Provincial Police, they were not awarded a permanent contract. Langsner decided to return to the stage to make some money. Gressner did not like the idea of "prostituting" his skills in cheap theatrical performances, so he withdrew from the partnership and returned to Honolulu.

Sometime in the spring of 1928, in Victoria, Langsner met Inspector William Frederick Hancock of the APP. Hancock was impressed by Langsner's stories of assisting police departments all over the world. A few months later, Hancock was officially put in charge of the Booher

Alberta Provincial Police assembled on the steps of the Edomton Courthouse in 1927. In the foreground, second from the left is Inspector William Frederick Hancock. Next to him, second from the right is Commissioner Willoughby C. Bryan. These two officers were responsible for bringing Dr. Otto Maximillian Langsner, an Austrian mind reader, onto the Booher case.

case. After repeated searches had failed to turn up the murder weapon, he remembered his meeting with the famous criminologist.

Willoughby C. Bryan, Commissioner of the APP, gave Hancock permission to contact the British Columbia Provincial Police. A superintendent replied that Dr. Langsner had indeed successfully carried out a minor assignment for the B.C.P.P. Based on that recommendation, the APP telegraphed Langsner, requesting his help with the Booher case. Langsner said he would be pleased to be of assistance, for a fee of $250. That was a hefty price in an age when the average working man's annual income was less than $1,000, but the Alberta police were getting desperate.

Langsner took the train to Edmonton, and met Hancock and Bryan on July 18. Exactly what was said in that interview would later be a matter of controversy. The two officers would testify that they specifically told Langsner they wanted him to find a rifle. Langsner would swear that he was instructed to locate "a missing piece of evidence." He would insist that the police never said a word to him about a gun.

Now that Langsner was officially on the case, Hancock accompanied him to Mannville to attend the preliminary hearing. Commissioner Bryan issued an order to his men that the criminologist from Vienna was to be given every assistance. Whatever had or had not been said in the interview, by the end of the hearing Langsner surely knew that the "missing piece of evidence" was a .303 Ross rifle.

After the preliminary hearing, Langsner told Hancock he believed Henry Booher hadn't said everything he knew in court. He said he wanted to meet Henry personally. That way he could "get close to him and feel his thoughts."

Henry Booher was staying at the Mannville Hotel, so Hancock took Langsner there. It was not a wise move. Henry was in the grip of a living nightmare; his wife and eldest son murdered, and his younger son the chief suspect! The last thing in the world Henry wanted to do was meet a man who professed to be a mind reader. When Hancock and Langsner entered his room, Henry seized the Austrian by the collar and the seat of his pants, and in a maneuver known to bouncers everywhere as "the bum's rush," threw him out! Dr. Langsner made no further attempts to "get close" to Henry Booher.

That humiliating experience did nothing to dampen Langsner's determination to solve the mystery of the missing rifle. He asked to be taken to the Booher farm. There he spent a few minutes walking around the deserted buildings, but did not go out to the fields. Later, Langsner would claim that on that visit he had an "impulse" to examine a clump of trees about 130 yards west of the barn. But if he had indeed had such a thought, he did not act on it at the time. Instead, he went to the Stephenson house.

Langsner stood for a long time with his hands on the rack from which the rifle had been stolen. Then he went to the cupboard where the box of shells had been kept, and repeated the laying on of hands. Satisfied that he had learned all that he could at that site, Langsner returned to Mannville in time to catch the train to Edmonton; the same train that was carrying Vernon back to the Edmonton jail.

The next morning, July 19, Langsner told Bryan and Hancock that he wanted to spend some time alone with Vernon. He explained that during the hearing he had been unable to "feel his thoughts properly" due to interference caused by feelings from all the other people in the room. The thoughts of Henry and Dorothy Booher had been especially distracting, he said. Bryan agreed to let Langsner see Vernon, but warned him that he was forbidden by law to question Vernon or discuss the case with him.

As a suspected mass murderer, Vernon was no ordinary prisoner. His jailers decided he could not be kept in the cells with the drunks and petty hoodlums who were their usual guests. Instead, he was locked up alone in a cell in the basement which was usually reserved for female prisoners.

When Langsner went downstairs he found Vernon sitting at a bare table in an anteroom. The doctor stayed only eight minutes. He told Bryan he had said nothing to the young man, only stared at him to absorb his thoughts. At one point, he said, Vernon asked him what he was doing, but he did not respond. Nor did he reply, he said, when Vernon asked if the police had found the rifle.

The next morning, July 20, Langsner returned to the basement of the Edmonton jail. He sat for a few minutes in front of Vernon's cell door, neither looking at the prisoner nor speaking to him. His sole purpose, he said later, was to absorb Vernon's feelings.

Now Langsner told the police he was ready to find that missing piece of evidence. Frank Lesley drove Langsner to Mannville. At four in the afternoon they reached the Booher farm.

Lesley wasn't quite sure what to make of the little Austrian criminologist. He apparently did not share his superiors' faith in Langsner's so-called psychic powers, but he had orders to assist him. Lesley's doubts were almost immediately justified when, instead of going straight to the place where the rifle was supposedly concealed, Langsner began to wander around, as though searching the ground; ground that had already been thoroughly combed several days earlier. (It must be kept in mind that Langsner would claim he'd had an "impulse" about a certain clump of trees on his very first visit to the farm. He had not acted on that impulse then, and he did not do so now — at least, not immediately.)

Lesley was right behind Langsner as he wandered around, and seemed not to have any real idea where to look. "He led and I followed right close at his heels. We looked around first in the grain fields, that is, just off north of the barn where Rosak was killed and then we zig-zagged all over that bit of terrain outside the west fence."

This must have been exasperating for Lesley. He, Fred Olsen, and volunteers had been all over that ground! Did this man know where the missing rifle was, or didn't he?

Langsner led Lesley through the west field, over a barbed wire fence into the farmyard, back into the field again, and then into bush. Lesley was beginning to think the whole exercise was a waste of time. Then they came to a place about 130 yards west of the barn. Here were several clumps of trees amidst patches of long grass and bare ground. Langsner moved from one clump to the next, closely examining every foot of ground. Then he said, "Ah, there it is!"

Looking over Langsner's shoulder, Lesley saw the rifle immediately. It lay on an open piece of ground that was surrounded by a few small trees and some thick grass. The gun was so plainly visible, it didn't seem possible that the earlier searchers could have missed it. But there it was: a .303 Ross rifle!

The weapon had supposedly lain on the ground, exposed to the elements, for ten days. Fingerprint testing produced only useless blotches. The police still could not prove Vernon Booher had used it to kill four people. But the gun was crucial to their case. Moreover, the police were firmly convinced that Dr. Langsner could help them get the truth out of Vernon Booher.

On July 22, Lesley went to the basement of the Edmonton jail and held up the rifle for Vernon to see. "This is the gun," he said. The once-confident Vernon turned pale. He asked Lesley what the white powder marks on the gun were. "To bring out any fingerprints," the policeman replied. Vernon asked, "Did you find any?"

Of course, Lesley did not admit there were no fingerprints. He turned around and left, letting Vernon sweat for awhile. Then Dr. Langsner paid Vernon another visit.

What exactly happened in the few minutes Langsner spent with young Booher is not known. Langsner wouldn't give direct answers about it during Vernon's trial, and nothing Vernon said about it could be verified. The only factual statement came from a constable who was on guard duty. He testified that at one point Dr. Langsner opened the door and asked for a glass of water for Vernon.

Shortly before noon, Langsner walked into Commissioner Bryan's office, where Bryan, Inspector Hancock, and Detective Lesley were waiting. He told them he thought Vernon was going to confess "in a little while," Langsner would deny that he had in any way specified a time at which the confession would be forthcoming. But the officers must have thought a confession was imminent, because they waited. At about one o'clock, Lesley received a message that Vernon wanted to talk to him. The detective went to Vernon's cell with a notebook in hand. When he emerged later that afternoon, Lesley had in shorthand notes what he claimed was Vernon's full confession.

> I want to get it all over with. I don't care if I hang tomorrow. I killed my mother as she sat at the table. And then I shot my brother Fred as he rushed into the house to see what had happened. The two of them were lying in the house when

Councillor Scott called. I don't know what I would have done if he had attempted to enter the house.

When Bill came in from the field, I shot him in the barn so that he would not find the bodies. Gabriel Gromley I shot in the bunkhouse. I had planned to sink his body in fifteen feet of water and throw the rifle in after him, but I did not have time.

Mother and Fred's constant nagging of me about a girl I am crazy about was the cause of the whole thing. I had it planned out for some time.

I am making this confession because I want to get it over with, and I don't want father and my sisters to have to appear in court.

The tale of how a foreign doctor with psychic powers had found the missing rifle and cracked one of the most baffling murder cases in Canadian history was a sensation. Langsner was still demonstrating his special talents on stage, and now he was playing to packed houses. Newspapermen sought him out to get his life story. He, or the lovely Madame Langsner, happily obliged. Milking the publicity for all it was worth, Langsner announced that he was willing (for a fee) to solve a mystery that had stumped Canadian police for almost a decade: the disappearance of Ambrose Small.

Toronto theatre tycoon Ambrose Small had vanished without a trace on the night of December 1, 1919. In spite of intense investigations, police had not turned up a single clue to the fate of the millionaire. The Small case, in fact, remains unsolved to this day.

However, Inspector Alfred Cuddy of the Ontario Provincial Police was not interested in Langsner's offer to locate Ambrose Small. Cuddy dismissed Langsner's claims of psychic powers as nonsense, and said that he "would not give thirty cents" for Langsner's help. The Toronto policeman also investigated some of Langsner's claims to being an internationally renowned criminologist, and received some disturbing replies.

The police in New York, Chicago, Montreal, and Vienna had never heard of Dr. Langsner. Neither had Scotland Yard. Sir Arthur Conan

Doyle not only denied that he had ever worked on a criminal case with Dr. Langsner, but also said the man was a total stranger. Clearly, Langsner had lied about his colourful past. But this only increased the public's curiosity about him, especially since he was about to play a key role in Vernon Booher's trial.

The trial began on September 24, 1928, in the Edmonton court-house, with Chief Justice W.C. Simmons presiding. Representing the Crown was veteran prosecutor Edward B. Cogswell, K.C. The first thing brought to Magistrate Simmons's attention was that Vernon Booher was not represented by legal counsel. (Henry Booher had refused to hire a lawyer.) Neil D. Maclean, an attorney with a reputation for championing underdogs in seemingly hopeless cases, was appointed by the court to represent Vernon. Maclean was assisted by J.D. Nicholson, a former APP Inspector with a sterling record as a criminal investigator.

In addition to the evidence submitted by police and other witnesses, Edward Cogswell had witnesses who related potentially damning statements Vernon had allegedly made while he was in jail. Constable Fred Olsen testified that Vernon told him, "I know who committed this crime, but I am not going to say a word about it." Olsen said he tried to press Vernon on the matter, but Vernon would say no more. Then in a sudden outburst the young man had asked, "Supposing a man was in love with a girl; his mother and sister did not want him to go out with that girl; that they threatened him that if he did not quit going with that girl, they would spread it all over the neighbourhood; what would you do?" Olsen also said that a while later, Vernon had told him that killing Rosak and Gormley had been a mistake.

Constable Henry Crane had been on guard duty July 16, when Henry Booher visited his son. Crane stated that after Mr. Booher left, Vernon said, "This has aged my father five years. If I had known that it would have caused so much grief, this would never have happened." Crane also testified that Vernon told him *he had never lost his temper before.*

These statements came from police officers who were hostile to Vernon. But the most damaging statement came from a man who was Vernon's spiritual advisor and was sympathetic toward him. Thomas Sutherland Stewart, a Salvation Army officer, had long been ministering to men in prison, including the condemned on Death Row. He had offered his services to Vernon, and the young man had willingly accepted. When called to the witness stand, Stewart made it clear that he did not wish to testify. He said anything that passed between him and Vernon was confidential, and he did not want to be a Judas. Vernon astounded the court by giving Stewart permission to speak freely. Reluctantly, Stewart testified that in one of their meetings Vernon had asked him, "Do you think that God can forgive me for my deed?" He also said Vernon told him he did not remember a thing about the night of the murders.

All this did not mean it was an open-and-shut case. Neil Maclean saw numerous weaknesses in the Crown's case. First, there was the rifle that police officers and a small army of searchers had failed to find, but then had been "discovered" by a so-called psychic. How could the searchers not have seen the gun, if that whole time it had been in the place where Lesley said Langsner found it? Maclean suggested that the police had planted the gun; that it wasn't even the same gun that had disappeared from Charles Stephenson's home. Stephenson was shown the gun the police claimed was the murder weapon. He testified that it resembled his missing rifle, but would not swear it was the very same gun. Cogswell said that the model of Ross rifle Stephenson owned was rare; finding one just like it would be difficult. J.D. Nicholson soon contradicted that. He found several guns of that very model in second-hand stores in Edmonton. Moreover, the police had been unable to positively identify the bullets and bullet fragments taken from the bodies as .303 calibre.

Maclean raised the issue of motive. So far, the police had been unable to establish any substantial reason for Vernon wanting to kill his mother and brother. Testimony from family members eventually revealed that the argument with Fred had been sparked when Fred sat in Vernon's car in greasy clothes. Henry had broken up the quarrel. Vernon, still in a temper, had jumped into his car and driven to Calgary, where he stayed until he ran out of money. He sold his car, paid someone five dollars to put a cast on his arm, and went home with the story that he'd wrecked his car in an accident. This was his way of gaining family sympathy. This bit of insight into relationships among the Booher clan still did not provide anything in the way of motive, but it did contradict the picture of family harmony painted by Henry and his daughters. It also suggested that Vernon was not mentally stable.

From Maclean's cross-examination of Dr. Heaslip, the court learned that on May 19, two months before the shootings, members of the Stephenson family had found Vernon lying on the ground near a team of horses. He seemed to be unconscious, but regained his senses enough to say a horse had kicked him. The Stephensons drove Vernon to the hospital where Dr. Heaslip examined him, and found nothing wrong. In the doctor's opinion, Vernon had faked the accident so he could get close to a nurse, identified only as Miss MacMillan, who worked at the hospital. Reporters in the courthouse noted that Vernon, who generally appeared cool and unconcerned during the proceedings, blushed when the nurse's name was mentioned.

Could Miss MacMillan have been the young woman Vernon had fallen for, but to whom his mother and siblings had objected? The sisters would testify that Miss MacMillan, or any other girl Vernon might have taken a liking to, would have been welcomed into their home. But Maclean was less concerned with the family's reaction to Vernon's alleged love interest, than he was with presenting yet another incident in which Vernon's behavior had not been that of a normal youth.

Maclean was venturing into new territory, as far as procedure in a Canadian court of law was concerned. He believed the greatest liability to the Crown's case was Dr. Otto Langsner. The lawyer wanted to examine the possibility that Vernon Booher had been under the influence of hypnotism.

At Maclean's request, the jury left the courtroom so they wouldn't be unduly influenced by statements that were not yet proven facts. Then Maclean called Dr. Edgerton Pope to the stand. Dr. Pope stated that the medical profession recognized a condition known as "post-hypnotic trance." He said individuals suffering from epilepsy or neurotic disorders were more likely than others to be influenced by a hypnotist's suggestions. Furthermore, he said, such a person could experience a condition called "epileptic automatism" and commit an extremely violent act, of which he would have no memory. Dr. Pope believed Vernon's unusual incident in the field, when the Stephenson's had found him, could have been a symptom of such a condition. It was entirely possible, the doctor said, that Vernon had suffered one major fit, and quite likely numerous minor ones that had gone virtually unnoticed. Pope explained that under hypnosis, such a person could be made to believe he had committed a crime of which he was actually innocent, and would even confess to the deed.

Cogswell challenged Dr. Pope's statements. He said many experts denied that a person under hypnosis could be made to do anything he or she would not do while conscious. Dr. Pope acknowledged the views of other experts, but said he did not agree with them.

This point of contention would be revisited several times in that Edmonton courtroom, by several qualified witnesses for. Those speaking for the Crown said that it wouldn't have been possible for Dr. Langsner to hypnotize Vernon in the courtroom, and even if he had hypnotized the young man in jail, the effect would have lasted only an hour or so. They argued that even under hypnosis, Vernon could not be made to confess to a crime he had not committed.

Those speaking for the defence insisted that Vernon had a "suggestible and hysteric" personality. He could be easily hypnotized, they said, and the post-hypnotic trance could last for weeks, perhaps even a year. As for the question of whether or not a hypnotized person could be made to do something he or she would not normally do, the explanations indicated that there were grey areas. In most instances, a man under hypnosis would not falsely confess to murder. However, he *might* be convinced to confess to a murder of which he was innocent, if he were told that by doing so he was protecting someone else, or was told that his lie, though fundamentally immoral, was nonetheless for a greater good.

With the jury still out of the room, Maclean called Dr. Langsner to the stand. The mentalist did not at resemble the impressive figure he did in his stage performances. His answers were evasive, and he seemed to have a rather foggy memory. Maclean asked him, "Is it a fact that you claim to be able to read, to exercise mental telepathy?"

Langsner replied, "They call it so."

"Reading another man's mind?"

"Yes," Langsner said. "They call it that, I presume."

"They call it telepathy?"

"Yes."

"Are you able to do that?" Maclean asked.

"Oh yes, if it is necessary."

"You can read another man's mind?"

"Oh, I presume so."

Magistrate Simmons decided to put this claim to the test. The judge asked if he were to concentrate his mind on something, could Langsner tell him what it was. Langsner replied, "Yes, but I am not a thought reader. When you concentrate your mind, I am able to take it, but not telling anything." Langsner failed to tell the judge what he was thinking about.

In later testimony, Langsner would insist that he was a skilled hypnotist, but there had been a misunderstanding over his abilities as a mind reader. "I am not a thought reader," he would say. "I am only a researcher in this line."

Opinions about Dr. Langsner's abilities varied considerably. Dr. Hans Gessner, brought all the way from Honolulu to testify, lauded Dr. Langsner as a genius; the best hypnotist in the world. He said Langsner could easily have used hypnotism and telepathy to influence so pliable a subject as Vernon Booher. Gessner claimed that he himself had carried out a little experiment right there in court, and caused Vernon to turn in his seat and look at him.

In contrast, Dr. James McKay of the British Columbia Medical Association recalled his interview with Dr. Langsner, and a demonstration of the self-styled criminologist's powers. He had not been impressed at all. In fact, Dr. McKay had dismissed Langsner as a fraud.

Neil Maclean drew a sharp reprimand from Magistrate Simmons when he said, "Your Lordship, I am endeavouring to find out if the Alberta Provincial Police made any investigation in this case, or left it all to Dr. Langsner." Simmons called the remark "not at all proper." But the judge felt there was sufficient cause for the court to consider if Dr. Langsner *could* have influenced Vernon Booher's decision to "confess." He would not allow the confession Vernon had made to Detective Lesley to be admitted as evidence, and forbade any witness or attorney to mention that confession in the presence of the jury.

Of course, there was much more to the trial than Dr. Langsner's role in the case. There were questions about the times people had heard gunshots, the directions the sound of gunfire had come from, and even the possibility that there may have been two gunmen. There was conflicting testimony about the cows Vernon was supposed to have been driving home when he claimed to have heard shots. Dr. Heaslip, Constable Milligan, and Holburn Taylor said there were no cows in the barnyard when they arrived. Henry, Algertha, and Dorothy Booher all testified that the cows were there. People who claimed to have seen Vernon riding his horse toward the Stephenson barn — allegedly on his mission to steal the rifle — could not agree on what he had been wearing. A Stephenson farmhand named Broma Telka said he had been on that trail about the time the others allegedly saw Vernon, but hadn't seen anyone.

The question of how the alleged murder weapon turned up in a spot that had already been thoroughly searched had not been resolved. There was also an undercurrent of suspicion that Vernon's father and sisters were not telling the whole truth about family relations. Throughout the trial Vernon seemed to be beyond calm; he appeared to be completely devoid of emotion.

As the hearings came to an end after four days of testimony, it seemed as though the jury would have a lot of points over which to deliberate, and would probably be out for quite some time. No one, not even Neil Maclean, realized that a brief exchange between Edward Cogswell and Inspector Hancock had caused the jury to reach a decision long before the last witness left the stand.

In his cross-examination of Hancock, Cogswell asked, "Do you know that the accused made a confession?"

"I do," Hancock replied.

The prosecutor asked, "What date would that be?"

"That would be on Sunday, the 22nd of July."

At that point Magistrate Simmons interrupted and said, "And I think that my ruling will still apply as to its inadmissibility."

Previously, all mention of Vernon's alleged confession had been made in the absence of the jury. Now, for the first time, the jury members heard that there had in fact been a *confession*! The judge's remark that he had ruled it inadmissible did not erase it from the jurors' minds. The rest of the trial seemed to be little more than a formality. What did it matter where the cows were that night or how the murder weapon had so conveniently turned up in a field?

On the morning of Friday, September 28, Chief Justice Simmons made his summary to the jury. He concluded with: "Gentlemen of the jury, you have now in your hands one of the most sensational murder cases in the history of the province, and I am certain that you will discharge your duties in keeping with the highest ideals of British justice."

To the astonishment of all, the jury took less than half an hour to find Vernon Booher guilty on all four counts of murder. When Magistrate Simmons asked Vernon if he had anything to say, the young man replied, "Only that I am not guilty." Simmons wept as he sentenced Vernon to be hanged in the provincial jail at Fort Saskatchewan on December 15, 1928.

The transcript of Vernon Booher's trial filled 400 typewritten pages. Neil Maclean went through it again and again, but not until December 4, 1928, did he notice the one point upon which he could make a demand for a new trial. The Appellate Division of the Provincial Court of Alberta agreed that the jury at Vernon's trial had heard information about a confession, without knowing anything about the circumstances under which the alleged confession had been made. Vernon was immediately removed from Death Row, and a new trial scheduled for January 21, 1929. Mr. Justice W.L. Walsh would preside.

A new jury heard all of the evidence that had been presented at the first trial, and once again a storm of controversy raged around Dr. Langsner. Did he hypnotize Vernon Booher? Was the Austrian criminologist a genius or a fake? For the first time, Vernon began to show signs of stress. Perhaps that was because in this trial, the jury was permitted to hear the statements he was alleged to have made to jail guards. The worst damage to Vernon's case came from the testimony of a new witness, Warden John McLean.

The warden said that on July 24, accompanied by a guard named Herbert Holt, he had visited Vernon's cell. He asked the newly arrived prisoner if he had a lawyer. Vernon replied, "I am not putting up any defence … I am pleading guilty to the charge."

McLean testified that Vernon told him he'd had a visit from his father. According to Vernon, Henry had said, "Son, if you know anything, you had better tell. Speak up!" Then, Vernon had told him, "I realized then that suspicion might fall on Dad, and I decided to tell, as I did not want my dad blamed for something he did not do."

McLean said that Vernon had told him he did not understand why he didn't feel worse about the deaths of his mother and brother. He did feel badly about killing Gromley and Rosak, because he'd had no quarrel with them. But he didn't care about his mother and brother. "His mother," said McLean, "had said something against the girl he was keeping company with."

Neil Maclean knew this testimony was devastating, and he subjected Warden McLean to a forceful cross-examination. He wanted to know why McLean had been so long in coming forward with the information. McLean said he had not mentioned it to anyone until after Vernon's conviction, thinking the case was done with. "I will know enough in the future to keep quiet," he said.

Later the guard, Holt, told the court that Vernon had said to him, "I am going to plead guilty because I do not want my sisters dragged into the witness box." Holt said that when he asked Vernon why he committed the murders, the young man replied, "I do not know. There must be something wrong with me."

On the morning of January 24, Edward Cogswell made his address to the jury. He acknowledged that the motive for the murders was vague, but also that one thing was clear: Vernon Booher had killed his mother, his brother, and the two hired hands. The statements he had made to jail guards, if taken on their own and out of context, could each have referred to almost anything. But examined collectively and in connection with other evidence, they were admissions of guilt.

In a last ditch defence maneuver, Neil Maclean once again portrayed Dr. Langsner as the sinister agent behind Vernon's supposed confessions. The police had a case based only upon weak circumstantial evidence, until Dr. Langsner and his hypnotic powers came into the picture. The rifle the Austrian had "found," Maclean reminded the jury, had never been satisfactorily identified as the actual murder weapon, and had obviously been planted.

Justice Walsh began his address to the jury at 2:15 p.m., and spoke until 3:55. In the course of reviewing all the evidence, he said of Dr. Langsner's involvement: "It is a most unfortunate thing that this man was imported into the case at all. I think that it is a very, very regrettable occurrence. I have no doubt that those who are responsible for it regret it now as bitterly as I do."

Walsh went on to the evidence of Warden McLean and Herbert Holt. "If you believe that the boy was telling McLean the truth when he made that statement," he said, "it is as clear and straight a confession of guilt as one could find anywhere."

This time the jury took five hours to reach a guilty verdict. Judge Walsh told the jurors he agreed with their decision. He sentenced Vernon Booher to the gallows, then bowed his head and said a prayer for the condemned man's soul. Vernon was sent back to Death Row in the provincial jail at Fort Saskatchewan.

While Vernon awaited his date with the hangman, he was given a psychological examination by Dr. James McKay. Vernon made another confession to the doctor, this version somewhat different from the one he had given the police. He told McKay that on July 8, the day before the murders, he was seized with an urge to kill. He told his family he was going to the Austin farm, but instead he rode to the Stephenson place and stole the rifle. On the ride back he saw Broma Telka in time to hide in the woods until Telka had passed. He stashed the gun in some brush before going home to have supper with his family.

The following evening, Vernon said, he was still possessed by the need to kill. After his sisters had left for Mannville, he got the rifle, went into the house, and blew his mother's brains out as she sat at the table. He felt no emotion.

Fifteen minutes later, Fred stepped through the kitchen door. Vernon had been waiting for him. He gunned his brother down without hesitation. Vernon said he felt no more regret over this murder than he had over killing his mother.

Vernon told McKay he then went into the yard and hid the rifle in tall grass. After Mr. Scott had come and gone, Vernon picked up the gun and killed Bill Rosak in the barn. An hour later, he shot Gabriel Gromley in the bunkhouse. He hid the rifle in tall grass again, and ran to the Ross house. Later, in spite of Constable Olsen and the other men, Vernon was able to pick up the rifle and throw it as far as he could into the farm's west field. How the gun disappeared for so long was never fully explained.

Crime historians studying the Booher case years later believed Vernon made this story up, just as he had made up the confession he gave Frank Lesley. If he had indeed been seized with an "urge to kill," why hadn't he shot down Broma Telka, the first person he saw after stealing the gun? If the urge to kill was so irresistible, why had he waited until he was alone on the farm with Eunice to shoot her?

An intriguing point raised by author Frank W. Anderson in his book *The Vernon Booher Murder Case* concerns Constable Henry Crane's testimony that Vernon stated he had never lost his temper before. Did Vernon steal the rifle in anticipation of a serious confrontation with his mother over an issue that had put him at odds with her? Had he intended to use the gun to intimidate Eunice, but then had lost his temper and shot her from behind? Had the other three victims been slain simply because Vernon had to hastily cover up matricide? Whatever really happened on that Alberta farm, Vernon took the truth to his grave.

Vernon Booher was hanged early on the morning of April 24, 1929. The night before his execution, Vernon took a parting shot at Dr. Otto Langsner. He told Neil Maclean that Langsner had never hypnotized him. Maclean repeated the story to the press:

He came to me in the cell, and told me he was a doctor and that he was there to help me. I thought he was sent by my friends, and I told him where he could find the rifle. I even drew a diagram for him, so that he could find it. I thought he was going to hide it, or throw it in the river … but he double-crossed me … Langsner is a fake. He couldn't hypnotize a sick chicken. He's a double-crosser, that's all.

Before Vernon was taken to the gallows, he refused a sedative. "I need no dope," he said. But he did ask the guards who bound him if they could leave one arm free, so he could "take a poke" at the hangman, Arthur Ellis. It will never be known if there was any truth to Vernon's story about Langsner. With the execution, the case was officially closed.

Having failed to convince the Ontario government to pay him to locate Ambrose Small, Dr. Langsner left Canada. His name appeared in Canadian newspapers once more: in September 1930 he was arrested in Poland on suspicion of involvement in devil worship. Polish police found that Dr. Langsner was well travelled. His passport showed he had been all over Europe, Asia, Africa, the Americas, and Australia. He had eighteen volumes crammed with newspaper clippings about his remarkable feats as a hypnotist and mentalist. Langsner told the Polish authorities he had been an advisor on criminology to the government of Chile, had solved the mystery of the death of Lord Carnarvon (discoverer of Tutankhamen's tomb), and that as a police investigator in Canada he had solved four mysterious murders.

# 11.

# LAROCQUE AND LAVICTOIRE:
## A POLICY OF MURDER

William J. Larocque, fifty-seven, and Emmanuel Lavictoire, fifty-one, were the best of friends. They lived in Cumberland County, on the Ontario side of the Ottawa River. Both men eked meagre livings from the soil. Lavictoire worked a market garden next to the Ottawa-Montreal Highway, a few miles east of the village of Rockland. His property was near a dirt road connected to the highway. Larocque had a farm about a mile down the road. The houses on both properties were little more than shacks, proof of the owners' poverty. Oddly enough, in March of 1932, Larocque owned a car that he had bought brand new on October 10, 1930. Lavictoire purchased a new truck just a week later. Neighbours would have been surprised if either of the pair had suddenly become the owner of even an old, beat-up Tin Lizzie. For *both* men to suddenly be the proud owners of spanking new vehicles was the cause of some serious gossip, which gave way to dark rumours about how the men had suddenly become so wealthy. It wasn't until the spring of 1932 that the residents of the Ottawa Valley community learned the truth. The story would go into the annals of Canadian crime as one of the most bizarre murder cases in the nation's history.

---

On the morning of March 18, 1930, William Larocque planned to thresh grain, or so he would explain later. He expected help from his friend,

Lavictoire. If all went as planned, Lavictoire would bring along another able-bodied helper, twenty-three-year-old Leo Bergeron. Larocque was worried that Bergeron might not come, even though the young man would certainly need the day's pay.

Leo Bergeron was described as a man of "limited intelligence." Larocque had formerly employed him as a farm hand. However, Bergeron complained to a friend that Larocque made him do too much dangerous work. So he'd quit, and gone to work for a neighbouring farmer named Eugene Morin. Nonetheless, Larocque had insisted that he needed Leo to help with the threshing. Leo reluctantly agreed to go. Morin just as reluctantly gave him permission.

On the morning of the 18th Bergeron went to Lavictoire's house, and walked with him to Larocque's farm. They arrived there at 7:45 a.m.; Larocque was waiting. He had a team of horses hitched to a threshing mill. The first job of the day was to haul the mill into the barn.

Emmanuel Lavictoire and William J. Laroque: Ottawa Valley farmers who murdered for insurance money.

At that moment Larocque's eldest son, Arnold, was at a neighbour, Alcide Deschamps's, farm. A very short time later the people in the Deschamps house heard someone crying for help. They looked out and saw Emmanuel Lavictoire running across the fields toward them. He was shouting that something terrible had happened, something to do with the horses. When Lavictoire arrived at the house he was almost breathless, and clearly distraught. He told Deschamps he had to come with him to Larocque's barn right away. Alcide, his son Aurele, and Arnold Larocque hurried back with Lavictoire.

As they approached the barn the party heard the noise of stomping, neighing horses accompanied by Larocque's shouting. When they reached the entrance, they saw a shocking sight. William Larocque was struggling with the team of horses at the rear of the threshing wagon, trying to pull them back. The horses plunged, kicked, and stomped wildly. Beneath their feet on the concrete floor was Leo Bergeron's bloodied body. As the Deschamps and young Larocque looked on, a hoof struck Bergeron on the head.

Lavictoire and the rescue party seized the threshing machine and pulled it out of the barn. The horses quieted down immediately. Young Larocque was baffled. The horses were old, and had never been anything but docile before, and now they obediently followed as he led them to the stable. Meanwhile, Alcide and Aurele Deschamps went to the battered Leo Bergeron.

The young man was in a frightful state. He was covered with blood, and caked with straw and dirt from the barn floor. The floor around him was soaked with blood, and the walls were spattered with it. Amazingly, Leo was still alive, but barely! Alcide Deschamps later said, "I heard him lamenting."

Aurele and Arnold got into Larocque's car and drove off to a nearby farm where Leo's father, Leon, was working. Alcide Deschamps told Larocque and Lavictoire that Leo seemed badly hurt, and shouldn't be moved until a doctor arrived. They agreed. They knew the police would be coming soon, and they wanted the doctor to see Leo right where the horses had trampled him. Larocque fetched a buffalo robe from the house and used it to cover the injured man. Deschamps ran to the home of another neighbour where there was a telephone he could use to call a doctor. Larocque and Lavictoire waited in the barn with Bergeron.

Arnold and Aurele soon returned with Leo's father. Leon looked at his son and saw that he was fighting for breath and still had a glimmer of life in his eyes. But before ten minutes had passed, Leo died without uttering a word. Leon pulled the robe over his son's face and walked out of the barn.

Larocque and Lavictoire were standing at a corner of the building. Old Bergeron asked them what had happened. Larocque said he had hitched the horses to the back of the threshing mill, because he wanted it pulled into the barn backwards. He did not want Leo to drive the team because the horses were "too wild." He said Leo had just walked into the barn when the horses suddenly bolted and trampled him.

Lavictoire backed Larocque's story. He said the threshing mill hit Leo, knocking him to the ground. Then the horses trampled the young man, and nobody could make them stop.

Bergeron did not believe them. Enraged, he shouted, "You killed the young Lamarche for his insurance, and now you have slain my son!"

Bergeron lunged at Larocque, but the strain had been too much for the old man. He stumbled, and had to lean against the barn to stay on his feet. For the moment he forgot about the men he had just accused of two murders, and broke down as grief overwhelmed him.

When he had composed himself, Bergeron went back into the barn and crouched beside his son's body. Lavictoire quietly slipped away. Soon Dr. Martin Powers arrived, along with an Ontario Provincial Police constable named Buck. Leon Bergeron immediately told them he believed Larocque and Lavictoire had killed his son.

Larocque told Dr. Powers the same story he had told Bergeron. The doctor was inclined to believe Larocque: the situation certainly *looked* as he had described it. Nonetheless, he felt that the unusual nature of Leo Bergeron's death called for an examination by someone more qualified. Dr. Powers called in Dr. R.D. Little, a pathologist from Ottawa.

Dr. Little examined the body where it lay in the barn, and then had it removed by an undertaker. He looked at the horses' hoofs, which were unshod. They were covered with blood. He told Larocque to show him his hands. The doctor would say later that Larocque's hands were "clean, for a farmer's hands, and evidently had been washed but a short time before."

Meanwhile, Constable Buck had searched the barn and found something that was very curious indeed. Lying on a beam, high up on the wall of the barn, was a pitchfork handle. The end where the prongs should have been was broken off. The surface of the beam on which the handle had been lying was thick with dust, but the handle had no dust on it at all. It had obviously been placed there very recently. Larocque said he knew nothing about the pitchfork handle. Dr. Little examined it closely and saw what appeared to be bloodstains.

Dr. Little took the pitchfork handle and some samples of blood-stained debris from the barn floor. Tests would show that in all cases the blood matched that of Leo Bergeron. The doctor did a post-mortem examination. He found major injuries to the head, especially the left side of the skull, which was crushed. Most of the damage could have been caused by blows from the horses' hoofs — but there was one fracture that did not seem consistent with the other injuries.

While Dr. Little was busy with his unpleasant task, two Ontario Provincial Police officers, Sergeant Harry Storey and Constable Harold Dent, were conducting their own investigation at Larocque's farm. They noted bloodstains on the walls quite a distance from where the horses had supposedly trampled Bergeron. Blood had also spattered on the walls, too high up to have come from a victim lying on the floor. Moreover, the straw, chafe, and other debris on the floor had been considerably disturbed where the trampling had taken place, but in other areas it had hardly been disturbed at all. A ladder in one corner of the barn had a freshly broken rung near the bottom, but there was no blood on it. Sergeant Storey asked Larocque how the rung had been broken. Larocque said he didn't know.

The threshing wagon was still in front of the doorway. In a drawer of the wagon the officers found a heavy steel wrench. It could easily be used to bash in a man's head. But there was no blood on the tool. Then Storey noticed the pump in the yard, just a few feet from the barn. Larocque could have clubbed Leo with the wrench, and then washed his hands and the murder weapon at the pump.

Storey remembered Leon Bergeron's angry accusations involving insurance. He asked Larocque if he had taken out any life insurance policies. Larocque said he had a $1,000 policy on his own life, a $1,500 policy on Arnold's life ... and a *$5,000* policy on Leo Bergeron!

There was nothing illegal about Larocque having a life insurance policy on Leo Bergeron. But why would he take out such a large policy on a neighbour, and a relatively small one on his own son? Why take out a policy on Leo at all? How did a man of Larocque's scant means meet the premium payments? Storey became even more suspicious when he learned that nobody else in the Larocque family, including Mrs. Larocque, knew anything about the insurance policies. Storey questioned Larocque again about what had happened that morning. The farmer stuck to his statement.

On March 19, Storey returned to Larocque's farm with several constables. He wanted to re-enact what had happened the previous morning. Larocque, pleased to oblige, had the threshing wagon placed in the position it had been in just before the supposed accident. One constable took the part of Leo Bergeron and stood at the head of the team of horses. Two others, representing Larocque and Lavictoire, stood at the tongue of the wagon. Storey gave the order to proceed.

The concrete floor at the barn entrance was about a foot higher than the ground. When the wagon wheels rolled over this obstacle, the wagon shot forward, bumping the horses from behind. The startled animals stomped and plunged for a few seconds, but then were quiet again. They began to nibble at some hay in a rack.

At that point Sergeant Storey was certain that Leo Bergeron had been murdered. But how to prove it? He got in touch with the Attorney General of Ontario's office in Toronto and asked for the best detective they could send. Inspector William H. Stringer was soon on his way to Cumberland County.

Stringer arrived on March 23, and collected all the information local police had. Like Sergeant Storey, Stringer quickly focused on Leon Bergeron's statement about insurance. He questioned local insurance agents and other potential witnesses, and was astounded by what he found. In June 1930, Larocque and Lavictoire had unsuccessfully tried to insure Leo Bergeron's life. A month later they found a new prospect, Athanase Lamarche. Athanase was about twenty-eight years old. Like Leo Bergeron, he was of lower than average intelligence.

Ontario Provincial Police Inspector William H. Stringer solved the Leo Bergeron murder case.

Larocque went to Harvey D. Cameron of the Manufacturers' Life Assurance Company and told him young Athanase Lamarche was a good prospect for a policy. It wouldn't have been unusual for Larocque to do this, because the insurance companies paid commissions to people who directed business their way. Larocque then went to Felix Lamarche, Athanase's father, and convinced him to take his son to see Mr. Cameron. The insurance agent sold the Lamarches a life insurance policy on Athanase, with Felix as beneficiary. The policy was for $2,000, with double indemnity, meaning the money paid to the beneficiary was doubled in case of accidental death. Felix paid the first premium of $62.50. Larocque and Lavictoire soon convinced Felix to increase the policy to $5,000 with double indemnity. In August, they talked Felix into taking out yet another $5,000 policy on Athanase, this time with the Northern Life Assurance Company. Felix was once again the beneficiary.

It was highly unlikely that Felix Lamarche had designs on his own son's life. In those days in rural Canada, older people depended on their adult children to look after them. In all probability, Felix had been persuaded into taking out the policies in case of some unforeseen tragedy, leaving him with no support in his old age. Moreover, if Athanase kept up the premium payments for twenty years, he would be able to cash in the policy and buy a farm of his own.

On the night of October 4, 1930, Athanese Lamarche was in a car with Larocque and Lavictoire on the Quebec side of the Ottawa River. Larocque, who was at the wheel, drove the car onto the ferry dock at the town of Masson. According to Larocque's own statement, Lamarche was sitting in the front beside him, and Lavictoire was in the back seat.

> On arrival at the wharf at Masson, I drove onto it stopping about 50 feet from the brow of the wharf. I also stopped the engine, pulled the emergency brake back, and left the lights on. This Ford is a model of 1924, and was in good working condition. I got out of the car and walked back a short distance, about 40 feet. When I got some distance back, I heard the car engine start, but I did not look back. In a few seconds, I did look back and saw the car going ahead. I followed up,

but did not reach the car, the car plunging into the Ottawa River. I looked over the side of the wharf and saw a man in the water. I tried to reach him the first time, but he went down. While he was down, I got up on the wharf and looked for something to reach him, could not find anything. I threw off my small coat, got down in the same position on a piece of projecting square timber, caught my coat with one sleeve with my left hand and held the wharf with my right; just as I swung, the man came to the surface, he grabbed my coat, and pulled on it, and I finally got him out. It was Lavictoire. Looked for the other man, but he did not appear.

Athanese Lamarche's body was found near the wharf the next day, but strangely, it was several feet *upstream* from where the car had gone into the water. No one had any explanation for how that could have happened. The only surviving witnesses to whatever had happened on the Masson wharf were Larocque and Lavictoire. Amazingly enough, no one in authority seemed to question this bizarre sequence of events — that within weeks of an insurance policy being taken out on his life, young Lamarche would be in a car that should suddenly start up, all by itself, and roll into the Ottawa River! Lavictoire said that Athanese started the car. If he did, why would he drive straight for the end of the dock? Why didn't Lavictoire stop him? And how was it that the only one Larocque managed to rescue was his pal Lavictoire? The events that followed also seemed to have escaped official scrutiny, but they certainly set the gossip mills turning.

The Manufacturers' Life Assurance Company gave Felix Lamarche a cheque for $10,000. The Northern Life Assurance Company refused to pay, on the grounds that the insurance application was incomplete. Larocque and Lavictoire actually went to the Northern Life office and demanded that the company pay Lamarche what was owed him, but to no avail. Lamarche deposited his $10,000 in the bank. Within six months it was almost all gone, straight into Larocque and Lavictoire's pockets.

Felix Lamarche was not a sophisticated man. He was a simple, uneducated farmer who was easily intimidated and duped. Soon after his son's death, Larocque and Lavictoire began demanding money from him. And he gave it to them. He later explained to investigators that these handouts were gifts. But it was more likely that the pair had browbeaten the old man into believing they could have the law on him for involvement in his son's death. They also swindled money out of him as an investment in a non-existent gold mine. They even tricked Lamarche, who was illiterate but could write his own name, into signing a couple of blank cheques.

Even as they were going through Lamarche's money, Larocque and Lavictoire were busy trying to set up their next victim. First, they tried to arrange life insurance for Leo Bergeron, with his father as beneficiary. Leon Bergeron knew nothing of this, and in any event the insurance companies refused the applications.

The pair dropped Leo as a prospect for the time being, and tried to lure two other victims into the snare. One was a young man named Harry Maylon, an immigrant from England with no family in Canada. The other was Henri Paquette, a seventeen-year-old orphan. Maylon and Paquette both smelled something fishy, and couldn't be drawn into the scheme. The conspirators turned back to Leo Bergeron.

On July 7, 1931, Larocque finally succeeded in getting La Societe des Artisans Canadienne Francais Insurance Company to write up a policy of $5,000 (with double indemnity, of course) on Leo Bergeron with Leon Bergeron named as beneficiary. Later Larocque had himself made beneficiary on the grounds that Leo worked for him, and if anything happened to Leo, he would be responsible for the expenses. Leon Bergeron knew nothing of the policy until later, and then he tried to talk his son out of it, because Leo couldn't afford the premiums. Leo said that was no problem, since Larocque was willing to pay them.

Due to some bureaucratic snags it took quite a while for the insurance contract to be completed. Larocque would later tell Inspector Stringer that Leo had been happy working with him, and was always asking him for extra work. In fact, just the opposite was true. Over the weeks Leo grew to dislike working for Larocque very much; to fear him, in fact. In November Leo had to borrow ten dollars from the bank. He'd been fined for public drunkenness in Hull, Quebec. The bank would loan the money to Leo, only if Larocque would sign as his endorser. Larocque constantly reminded Leo that now he was indebted to him.

In mid-January 1932, Bergeron went to work for Eugene Morin. Morin had no money to pay Leo, but if the young man was willing to work for room and board through the winter, he might be able to earn some money in the spring and summer. That suited Bergeron, but it did not get Larocque off his back about the money he owed the bank. That month Leo had to renew the note at the bank, and again he had to get Larocque to sign for him. A short time later Leo was able to pay off five dollars, but the bank manager told him he would have to pay the remainder very soon. Larocque also told Leo that if he didn't pay the debt on time, Constable Dent would put him in jail. Larocque actually paid off the remainder of the debt, but didn't tell Leo, leaving the youth with the worry that the bank could send a constable after him at any time.

Then Larocque and Lavictoire told Leo he could get work cutting ice on the Ottawa River. They approached a man named Arthur Prevost who had an ice-cutting business, and suggested he hire Leo Bergeron. Cutting ice on the river was extremely dangerous, even for an experienced man. Prevost said he could not take on an untrained lad like Bergeron. Larocque and Lavictoire went back to Prevost several times to argue the point, and each time he refused. They went to Prevost's wife and asked her to speak to her husband about Leo. That didn't work, either. Then they went to Morin, and told him he should prevail upon Prevost to take Leo out on the ice with him. The suspicious Morin refused.

Of course, Larocque and Lavictoire were less interested in Bergeron earning wages than they were in him having an "accident" out on the river. Then they could cash in on a nice insurance policy. They had gotten away with their first act of murder so easily, it didn't even seem to occur to them that later their actions would seem awfully suspicious to the police.

Larocque and Lavictoire finally gave up on the ice-cutting plan and decided they would lure Bergeron back to Larocque's farm. Larocque told Leo he needed him for threshing. The lad *owed* him that much at least. But Leo wouldn't go. Day after day either Larocque or Lavictoire, or sometimes both, would show up at Morin's farm to try to persuade Leo to help them. Leo took to hiding whenever he saw either of them approaching. He would beg Morin to say he was away.

After a few days of this, Morin refused to lie for Bergeron. When Larocque showed up, Morin told him he had given Leo a choice; to work full time for him and him alone, or to get out and go to work for someone else. Larocque left. Leo told Morin he would not go to thresh grain for Larocque. He knew something terrible would happen to him if he went back to that farm. One day, Morin confronted Larocque on the matter. "Look here," he said. "You don't really want this young man to thresh. What is it you are really trying to get hold of him for? Out with it!"

Larocque angrily said he wanted Bergeron to help him with the threshing, nothing more. He and Morin exchanged heated words, and then Larocque left. The next day Larocque returned, and in a much more friendly tone he told Morin he wanted Leo for just two days. In return, Larocque would send two men to help Morin with *his* threshing when the time came. Morin passed this on to Bergeron, but Leo was immoveable: he would not go to Larocque's farm.

A day later, Lavictoire took another stab at it. He went to Morin's and told Leo a certain girl had been phoning his place looking for him. (Morin didn't have a telephone.) He said Leo had better come along with him to call the girl and see what she wanted. But Leo wasn't buying that one, either. Lavictoire left in frustration.

But he was back the next day, two or three times. Then Larocque came again. Finally, on March 17, Leo agreed to go the next morning. Whether he gave in at last out of concern over the debt, or because Larocque and Lavictoire simply wore him down, will never be known. Morin told Leo he did not have to go. But on the morning of the 18th, Leo did some chores for Morin before going with Lavictoire to Larocque's farm. Morin never saw Leo alive again.

Inspector Stringer had no doubt that Larocque and Lavictoire had murdered Leo Bergeron. But so far all of the evidence was circumstantial. The victim *could* have been trampled to death by the horses, but that didn't seem likely. Witnesses stated that there was nothing wild about Larocque's old horses. An expert on animal behavior said it would be very unusual for horses to stomp a man lying on the ground.

Then Stringer spoke to Elie Lalonde, the man who actually owned the threshing mill they'd been using. The mill was run by a gasoline engine that only Lalonde could operate. He told Stringer that Larocque had told him to come out to his farm at *noon* for the threshing, not in the early morning. Lalonde said he was surprised by this, because he had helped Larocque with threshing many times in the past, and never had he been asked to come as late as noon.

That Larocque and Lavictoire were so confident that they had committed the perfect crime and could not be caught worked in Stringer's favour. They were so sure of walking away from this one with yet another handsome payoff, that they freely gave statements to Stringer. There was no coercion, so everything they said would be admissible in court. Larocque and Lavictoire not only answered Stringer's questions, they volunteered a lot of information. They told him all about the insurance policies, about being on the dock when Athanase drowned, and about being at the barn when Leo was killed. The statements were full of contradictions and lies, and Stringer knew it. On April 5, less than a week after taking their statements, Stringer had Larocque and Lavictoire arrested on charges of taking money from Felix Lamarche under false pretences. That would hold them until he could find solid evidence to have them tried for murder. That was not long in coming.

Dr. E.R. Frankish of Toronto was a forensics expert retained by the Department of the Attorney General of Ontario. He had been involved in numerous high profile murder cases throughout the province. He was sent to Cumberland County to conduct his own post mortem on the remains of Leo Bergeron, independent of the one done by Dr. Little. Dr. Frankish found something that had been missed by earlier examiners; tiny pinprick wounds in Leo's groin, abdomen, hands, and wrists. There were also small puncture wounds on one eyelid, at the corner of the mouth, and inside one ear. Dr. Frankish concluded that these wounds had been inflicted with a pitchfork. Noting the bruises and abrasions on the head and body, the doctor reported that those injuries were not caused by horses' hoofs, but by blows from a blunt instrument, such as the handle of a pitchfork, and a sharp-cornered object, such as a wrench. He also determined that Leo had been struck at least thirty-seven times.

On the last morning of his life, Leo Bergeron had done some chores with Eugene Morin before setting out for the Larocque farm. He and

Morin had washed their hands and had dried them on the same towel. Morin told Stringer that Leo had no cuts, punctures or any other kind of injuries on his hands at that time. He would have noticed them.

The doctor and the detective pieced together a scenario of what probably happened that March morning. When Bergeron arrived with Lavictoire, Larocque already had the threshing wagon in front of the barn door, with the horses hitched to it. The wagon would block the interior of the barn from view, in case anyone should happen by. Larocque would have used some pretext to send Leo into the barn, perhaps telling him to close the cow shed door.

Once Leo was in the barn, he was doomed. One of the men attacked him with the pitchfork, stabbing at his abdomen and groin. Leo would have instinctively doubled over to protect his stomach and pelvic area. While the young man cried in pain and begged them to stop, the killers closed in on him, stabbing with the big fork and battering him with the wrench. One prong of the fork pierced Leo's left ear, and while trying to ward off blows to his head he was stabbed in the hands and wrists. Flying blood hit the walls. Somehow, during the swirl of violence, the rung on the ladder was broken. At last, a solid blow from the wrench cracked the left side of Leo's skull and he sank to his knees. Another bone-crushing strike to the same spot all but finished him.

Now the killers washed their hands and the wrench, and put the murder weapon away. They hid the pitchfork handle on the beam, not expecting for a moment that a policeman would look there. Whatever became of the iron prongs is not known. Then, while Lavictoire rushed across the field to get help, Larocque drew the team of horses into the doorway and whipped them into a frenzy so witnesses could see them trampling poor Leo.

On April 27, 1932, William Larocque and Emmanuel Lavictoire were committed to stand trial for the murder of Leo Bergeron. Because of a flu epidemic, the proceedings did not get underway until the winter assizes. It began on December 5, 1932, in the town of L'Original, the seat of Cumberland County, in a packed courthouse. The trial was in English, but some of the testimony was in French and had to be translated. Throughout the ten-day event, Larocque sat almost motionless, his face like stone. Lavictoire, on the other hand, was a fidgeting, nervous bundle of anxiety. On December 15, after deliberating for almost six hours, the jury reached a unanimous guilty verdict. Neither prisoner flinched when the judge, Mr. Justice Kerwin, sentenced them to hang on March 15, 1933. But when they were taken back to the jail and placed in their cells, Lavictoire fell apart and began to cry and protest his innocence.

At two o'clock in the morning, on March 15, 1933, three days short of a year from the date of Leo Bergeron's murder, Lavictoire was taken from his cell and hanged on the gallows in the L'Original jail yard. He did not go easily. Minutes later Larocque, maintaining his composure to the very end, was dropped to his death. This closed one of the strangest murder cases in Canadian history, in which the killers had tried to frame a pair of animals.

# 12.

## BILL NEWELL:
### THE SILK STOCKING MURDER

Hugh William Alexander Newell was the full name of the air-forceman at the centre of one of Toronto's most sensational murders. He went by Bill because he thought his first given name "sounded too sissy." Newell was born in Toronto in 1914, and by 1940, the year he committed murder, he'd had a somewhat checkered career.

As a youth, Newell had the potential to succeed academically, but since he wouldn't apply himself and frequently skipped school, had poor grades. Newell was a promising athlete; he especially excelled at the pole vault. While he was a student at Scarborough Collegiate Institute, he was considered for the 1936 Canadian Olympic team.

Young Newell's physical prowess wasn't matched by a sense of good sportsmanship, though. He was a show-off whenever he won an event, and a poor loser when he didn't. He lacked self discipline, and resented any form of authority. When he wanted to, Newell could be quite charming, and he was meticulous about his clothing. Nonetheless, many who knew him thought there was something devious about Bill Newell.

As he grew into manhood, Newell showed a tendency to be shiftless. He could not hold down a job for any length of time. He'd occasionally find odd jobs, but often he just went on relief. He made money illegally as a bookie at the race track and for prize fighting, and by playing poker. On the street he was known as Toots. Newell had a reputation as a tough guy and a bad man to cross. However, friends said that silver-tongued Toots could always talk his way out of trouble.

Newell was handsome and charismatic, and had an eye for pretty girls. He especially liked young women who were willing to support him financially. He was a persuasive liar, and told the young women he met very little about his background. Eventually they would discover his explosive temper and tendency for violence. Then, fear would dominate the relationship until it finally ended.

Newell married his first wife, Winnifred Moores, in 1934. They had a daughter named Doreen. By the time of their divorce early in 1938, Newell was living with another woman, Aune Marie Paavola. Bill and Aune had a six-month-old son named Billie. Three weeks after his divorce was finalized, Newell married Aune. If the young bride thought that her new husband was going to provide a home and security, she was in for a big disappointment.

Aune was born in Finland in 1917, and emigrated to Canada at the age of six. Her father, Urho Paavola, a widower, was unable to look after his daughter by himself, so he entrusted her to the care of a Canadian family in Bond Lake (now part of the Toronto suburb Richmond Hill). They were kindly people who made sure that Aune attended school and was cared for, even though Urho wouldn't let them formally adopt her. When Aune was fourteen her father remarried, so she went to live with him and her stepmother in Toronto. She grew up to be a vivacious, outgoing young woman whose dark haired beauty led friends to call her Spooky.

Aune and Newell became acquainted at the Finnish Social Club in Toronto. She often went there for the dances and other activities. Newell had been taken there by a Finnish friend to participate in athletic competitions. When the two started dating, Aune was likely unaware of Newell's marriage to Winnifred.

Newell would later claim that he married Aune only because of the baby. He said that when Aune learned she was pregnant, she wanted to have an "operation." (The word *abortion* was taboo in those days.) He said he couldn't have allowed such a thing to happen. A former roommate of Aune's would testify that Newell actually tried to convince Aune to have the abortion, but she had insisted on having the baby and getting married.

Aune soon learned that married life with Bill Newell was not easy. She had to work at low-paying waitressing and housekeeping jobs to support the family. Sometimes she had to turn to her father for financial assistance. This had also been Winnifred's experience.

Not long after he married Aune, Newell met another Finnish girl, Elna Lehto. In January 1940, Newell abandoned Aune and Billie, and moved in with Elna. One week later, Newell went off on an adventure to Finland.

This was the "Phoney War" period of the Second World War, when the conflict between the Allies and Nazi Germany seemed stalled in a stand-off, but Stalin's Soviet army had invaded. In Canada, a Finnish Relief Fund was established to send volunteers and other aid to the Finns. Newell contacted the organization's Toronto committee and said that he was willing to go if his travel expenses were paid. The Finnish consulate in Toronto made the necessary arrangements for him, even cutting through some red tape concerning his passport.

Newell informed the Toronto newspapers that he, a home-grown Canadian boy, was off to Finland to fight the Russians. As he told the reporters sent to interview him, "I tried to get into the Canadian army and they didn't need me, so my next choice of wars was the one that's going on over in Finland." This was not true: Newell hadn't tried to enlist in the Canadian army.

When Newell boarded a train in Toronto for the first stage of his long trip to Finland, reporters and photographers from the city's three major newspapers were there to see him off. The *Evening Telegram* reported:

> Bill Newell, 26-year-old Toronto lad, is leaving with the fighting Finns, because he likes Finns and "never did have any use for bullies." He is married to a Finnish girl and said: "I have lived among Finnish people here in Toronto for a long time and I understand them. That's one reason why I am willing to fight for them." His Finnish comrades-at-arms are hugely delighted that he has joined them.

The Finnish girl to whom the writer said Newell was married was not Aune. In a photograph that appeared in all three newspapers, the "pretty wife" Newell was kissing goodbye was Elna. Aune was deeply upset by the picture.

Two months later, Bill Newell was back in Toronto. He told the press tall tales about coming under Russian bombardment on his first day in Finland. He said that he had been wounded in the eye and the arm, and that he had refused to serve under the Nazi officers Germany had sent to assist the Finns.

Documents from the office of the Chief Registrar of American and Canadian Volunteers to Finland tell a different story. According to that evidence, Newell was a trouble maker from the moment he arrived in Finland. He refused to sign any agreement to serve in the war, and tried to induce other men to do the same. He had to be deported to Sweden, then Norway, and finally back to Canada. Newell later said that his real reason for going to Finland was to visit Elna's father, who lived in a war zone that was closed to travellers. Amazingly, Newell would claim that the Finnish government had decorated him and made him a commissioned officer as a reward for his distinguished service. He also said he had written articles about life in Finland for a British newspaper, the *Manchester Guardian*; another lie.

Once he was back in Canada, Newell somehow convinced the Finnish consulate to pay him twenty dollars a week until he could find a job. Five weeks later, he found work with the Dominion Bridge Company. He was soon off on workmen's compensation, though, because of an alleged injury. Then, on August 26, Newell took the big step so many other Canadian men were taking: he joined the armed forces. He signed up for the Royal Canadian Air Force, and was sent to Brandon, Manitoba, for training.

Now that Newell had regular income, Winnifred and Aune both demanded support for their children. Elna had no legal claim to any of Newell's money, because he was still married to Aune. Newell had to find ways to avoid giving anything to either of his wives. In order to be nearer to Toronto, he had himself transferred to the RCAF base at St. Thomas, Ontario. He arrived there in the third week of September and immediately applied for leave so he could clear up his marital problems.

Divorce proceedings between Newell and Aune had been initiated months earlier, but had stalled because lawyers' fees made divorce rather expensive. Aune had also temporarily withdrawn her consent until she fully understood where she and her little boy stood. She was determined that Newell would meet his financial responsibilities toward the child.

During the last week of September, Newell spent a lot of time with Aune, trying to convince her to come to a private agreement. He wanted her to give him custody of Billie, whom he would then leave in Elna's care while he was serving in the RCAF, making Elna the boy's legal guardian. She would therefore be eligible for the "dependent's allowance" Newell would be obliged to pay. Aune would still receive the money she was due as his legal wife, but he wanted her to "kick back" twenty dollars a month to him, supposedly to help pay for the child's support.

Aune would not agree to any of this. She wanted to keep custody of Billie, and receive support payments from Newell. When it became clear to Newell that Aune would never budge, he decided on a more drastic course of action; one that would leave him with the child, his money, and the freedom to marry Elna.

———————————

While he was in Toronto, Newell stayed at Elna's home at 172 Howland Avenue. He didn't always spend the night there, which didn't surprise Elna: Newell often stayed out all night. She would later state that Newell was not home on the night of Tuesday, September 24, and probably not the night of the 25th, either.

Newell would later admit that on Wednesday, September 25, he went to Centre Island. There was nothing unusual about that. People who weren't island residents took the ferry over to enjoy the parkland all the time. But Newell would have noticed, as he strolled through the maze of woodlands and waterways, that many of the cottages had been closed for the season, and there were relatively few visitors. Some parts of the island were actually quite isolated.

Newell's meetings with Aune were usually quite cordial. She still felt affectionate toward her wayward husband, and apparently believed that she could persuade him to do what was right for her and Billie. On Saturday, September 28, Newell spent the night at 15 Grange Avenue, where Aune lived with her roommate, Orvokki Hakamies. Billie was living with Aune's aunt in Vineland, near St. Catharines, at the time.

At eight o'clock on the morning of Sunday, September 29, Newell went home to Elna. He told her that he had spent the night in the Toronto military barracks. Three hours later he was back at Aune's flat.

Newell had made arrangements to take Aune and Orvokki to a concert that evening. Now he said that he wanted to take Aune out to lunch. They left the house at 1:30 p.m., and Aune told Orvokki she would be back in an hour.

Aune's landlady, Mrs. Toini Ranpors, saw the couple leave the house. She hadn't seen Newell in his RCAF uniform before, so she went out to the verandah to watch them. Mrs. Ranpors would later testify that Aune and Newell walked east on Grange Avenue, and then turned south on Beverly Street toward Queen Street where she lost sight of them.

Later that day, at 8:30 p.m., Newell met Orvokki and Mrs. Ranpors on Beverley Street. Orvokki said that Aune hadn't returned home, and she didn't know where she was. Newell said that he had parted with Aune at Yonge and Adelaide Streets after lunch, and he hadn't seen her since. He then went home to Elna.

The following day, Newell returned to the St. Thomas air force base. He went to the paymaster and asked an odd question: "How would a guy go about getting an allowance for a common-law wife?" On Tuesday, Newell wrote a letter to Aune, the only letter he was ever known to have written to her. In it he expressed his disappointment that she had not met him on Sunday night. Then he addressed the matter of Billie:

If you won't see me, at least write me out a paper signing Billie over to me. You said that I could have him so why go back on your bargain. You know your boyfriend doesn't want to be bothered with someone else's child. Elna is quite willing to be a mother to Billie and so will you please do as you agreed and see that it is fixed up for me to have him … Now you are acting as you are I don't consider you to be everything you should be to be Billie's mother. In your heart you know you don't want him, and I do and have always wanted him.

In the letter, Newell also said he wanted to get the divorce over with. There was a line that intimated that Aune wanted to talk about the two of them getting back together, but Newell wrote that it was useless because he loved Elna. Then he suggested that Aune get in touch with him:

You have my phone number so you can call me if you wish. I'll be in Toronto next week-end perhaps. Call me on the Saturday any time or perhaps I'll call you Saturday night. If you don't wish to call me on the phone write me and let me know your intentions as I want to get everything settled.

Before closing, Newell added a patriotic note. "I like it here in the Air Force and feel proud to be wearing my country's uniform." Curiously, Newell addressed the letter not to Mrs. Aune Newell, but to Aune Paavola. Newell wrote the letter for the benefit of the police. Aune would never read it. She was already dead.

Newell posted the letter in St. Thomas on October 1st or 2nd. It was delivered to 15 Grange on Thursday, October 4. The police were already looking for Aune, because on Tuesday evening Orvokki had reported her missing.

Newell obtained a forty-eight-hour leave and arrived back in Toronto on the evening of October 4. Elna told him that Aune's disappearance had been reported on the radio. Newell decided to contact the police right away.

At about 1:15 on the morning of October 5, Newell told Detective Sergeant Fred Skinner that Aune was not missing. She was hiding to avoid being served with divorce papers by his lawyer. Newell said that when he last saw Aune on Sunday evening, at Yonge and Adelaide, she had gone off with a boyfriend, another airforceman.

Newell took the opportunity to tell the detective that he had sent a letter to Aune a couple of days earlier. When Skinner said that Aune must have received it, Newell replied that she couldn't have if she'd been missing for a week.

Newell said that the letter had to be at 15 Grange Avenue, but he doubted if Aune's roommate would give it to him. Skinner wrote in his notebook that Newell said Orvokki "had no use for him."

After his talk with Detective Skinner, Newell returned to Elna's place. Skinner already thought that Newell seemed a little too anxious to bring the letter to police attention. Neither he nor Newell were aware that investigators had already seen the letter.

Later that morning, Newell phoned Orvokki and asked if Aune had shown up. He asked about the letter, and Orvokki agreed to give it to him. Then he called the restaurant where Aune had been employed to ask if anyone there had seen her. When he was finished with that part of his performance, Newell went to Toronto's Number 2 Police Station. At his suggestion, three detectives escorted him to 15 Grange to get the letter. Once he saw the document in police hands, Newell gave the detectives a list he had made of the names of men he believed were Aune's boyfriends.

Newell left the police at about 4:30 that afternoon and started for home. On the way he met an RCAF officer, Ernest Gilbert. Newell told Gilbert about his situation. Gilbert contacted RCAF brass and arranged for a ranking officer to accompany Newell to Number 2 Police Station that evening, and speak to the police on his behalf. The meeting lasted from eleven o'clock in the evening until well into the small hours of the morning of Sunday, October 6. Newell didn't return to Elna's until after three o'clock.

Later that day, Newell and Elna went to his mother's home for lunch. Then they had friends in for afternoon tea at 172 Howland. At five o'clock, Newell was about to leave for St. Thomas, when Detectives

William Mace and Frank Wilson arrived with stunning news: the police had found Aune's body. They took Newell and Ella in for questioning. Later, both were placed under arrest.

The body of Aune Paavola Newell , covered with a coat and partly hidden by brush, on an isolated part of Toronto Island.

At about one o'clock that Sunday afternoon, a Parks Department employee named Harry Lemon was making his rounds on Centre Island. Because there had been some complaints about poison ivy, he examined the paths more closely than usual. Not far from the island's filtration plant, a little footbridge connected the main part of Centre Island to a smaller bit of land called Mugg's Island, in one of the inner lagoons. Mugg's Island was undeveloped and quite overgrown. Near a seldom-used shoreline footpath, Lemon spotted pieces of tissue paper caught on some stalks of white clover. The undergrowth leading to this litter seemed to have been beaten down. Lemon looked further, and found a woman's shoe. He stated later:

> If it hadn't been for this shoe catching my eye I'd never have found the body. I saw it just off the path in the bushes – a woman's black shoe, almost new. As I parted the bushes to reach it I saw another shoe about five feet further on. Just past this second shoe a woman's fancy pencil glinted. As I straightened from picking it up, something white farther on caught my eye. It was a white tissue handkerchief caught on a weed.
>
> Farther on I found part of a garter, then a purse, next a stocking. The trail led right through the dense bush and rushes to the body. There was no path, but I could see where the weeds and long grass had been pressed down as the body was dragged. I knew at once it was a body. I knew I mustn't touch it for fear of disturbing evidence, so I returned to the Police Station and notified P.C. Agnew.

John Agnew, the constable on duty at the island's little police station, went to the scene with Lemon. In a thickly overgrown spot, he saw the body of a woman lying on its right side. The arms were doubled beneath the chest, and the legs were drawn up. It was covered with a black coat and large pieces of willow, dogwood, and sweet clover. Agnew removed only enough of the covering to see the face. It was purple, with clots of blood at the eyes and mouth. The constable left Lemon to guard the crime scene while he went back to telephone Toronto police headquarters.

Soon there were a dozen detectives and constables swarming over the crime scene, under the direction of Patrol Sergeant Albert Lee. The Coroner, Dr. John Laxton Watson, and a pathologist, Dr. Isaac Erb, examined the body. The woman had apparently been strangled with one of her own silk stockings. It was knotted so tightly, that the neck was constricted to almost half its normal size. There were also some marks and scratches on the face and legs.

The police concluded that the woman had been killed several yards from the place where her body was found, and then dragged to the hiding place. A thorough search of the area turned up an empty handbag, some pieces of tarred marline hemp cord, a lipstick and compact (which had been tossed into shallow water), some torn up pieces of a YMCA envelope with RCAF insignia, and a hat that was later identified by Orvokki as one she had loaned to Aune. Several blue woolen threads found near the body and along the trail were of particular significance.

*City of Toronto Archives, Globe and Mail Collection*

Parks Department employee Harry Lemon discovered the body while picking up litter and looking for poison ivy.

There was no identification on the body, but police had a good idea whose it was: the clothing matched the description Orvokki had given them when she reported Aune missing. In the Toronto morgue, Orvokki and Mrs. Ranpors identified the body as that of Aune Paavola. A little later, identification was confirmed by the grief-stricken Urho Paavola.

On October 8, a Finnish service was held for Aune in a funeral home. Newell was present, with police guards. Through most of the service, he looked at the floor, trying not to make eye contact with Aune's father or any of her friends. At the burial in Mount Pleasant Cemetery, he covered his face with his hands most of the time.

As a result of their investigation, the police came up with a scenario of what happened on the day of the murder. After turning off Grange Avenue onto Beverly Street, Newell and Aune went to the Active Service Canteen where, at about two o'clock., they had a quick lunch. Then they walked down to the ferry docks to catch the 2:50 boat to Centre Island. It was a lovely, sunny day, and Newell suggested to Aune that they could have a pleasant afternoon together and talk things over, before going back to pick up Orvokki for the concert. A week earlier Newell had told Aune on the telephone that he would like her to come and live with him in St. Thomas. She had no intention of doing so, but may have thought that she could persuade Bill to do what was best for their son.

Aune and Newell boarded the ferry *Sam McBride*, and ten minutes later they got off on Centre Island. The dock was a twenty-minute walk from the site he had chosen for the crime. The couple would have strolled along two main island streets, Manitou and Iroquois, before arriving at the footbridge to Mugg's Island. Then Newell lured Aune to what he thought was the perfect place for a murder.

The location was rarely visited, especially after the summer season. It was overgrown and almost invisible. In the tall weeds, a body could lie undetected for months.

As they followed the path along the lagoon, Newell might have tried one last time to convince Aune to sign the agreement he had been trying to press upon her for days. When she refused, Newell attacked her from behind. He seized her in a wrestling hold, putting pressure on her ribs near the heart, causing her to black out. While she was unconscious, he removed her shoes and stockings, probably to make the assault look like a sex crime. Then he strangled her. At some point during her struggle, Aune had inflicted a three inch scratch on Newell's cheek.

Once he had choked the life out of his victim, Newell concealed the body. He removed any identification from Aune's purse, and scattered the rest of the contents. Newell also took three objects from the body that might have been of use to the police in identifying the corpse: a brooch, a watch, and a signet ring with the initial *A*. Investigators never found these items, which Newell likely dropped in Toronto Harbour.

Newell covered his wife's body with her coat and some brush, never thinking for a moment that it would be discovered in a matter of days. Then he walked to the Centre Island docks and caught the 4:30 ferry back to the city. He made a stop at the military depot on the Canadian National Exhibition grounds, before going to 15 Grange Avenue to "keep" his concert date with Aune and Orvokki.

Newell denied having anything to do with Aune's murder. But there were flaws in his alibi, and the police thought the whole business with the letter seemed phoney. Moreover, they had some compelling circumstantial evidence. In the basement of Elna Lehto's residence they found pieces of rope similar to the one retrieved from the murder site. The rope wasn't the kind that was commonly found in Toronto hardware stores, and was therefore significant. The police thought Newell might have planted it on the island in advance, and could have used it to strangle Aune before he tied the silk stocking around her neck. They also found the same kind of sand, seeds, and decayed vegetation on Newell's boots that was at the crime scene.

Even more interesting to investigators was Constable Agnew's statement that he had seen Aune at the ferry docks on the afternoon of the murder. In a police lineup, he identified Newell as the man who had been with her. Newell had been reluctant to stand in line with eleven other uniformed airmen. "Why the hell should I?" he growled. "This is a goddamn frame-up!"

At the preliminary hearing, which opened on November 18, 1940, a magistrate determined that there was enough evidence for Newell to be tried for first degree murder. Throughout the hearing, Newell made outbursts as witnesses gave evidence, and had to be forced to desist. The trial was set for February 24, 1941. Even with the steady stream of discouraging war news that filled the media, the case that the newspapers dubbed "The Silk Stocking Murder" became a sensation.

J.W. McFadden, K.C., prosecuted for the Crown, and Goldwin C. Elgie, K.C., led the defence. The Honourable Mr. Justice Makins presided. The trial lasted nineteen days. Elgie dismissed the Crown's whole case as "circumstantial evidence in the raw." He accused the Toronto police of attempting to frame Newell. Elgie argued that the very idea of a man taking his estranged wife to a lonely spot for "flirtation" was ridiculous. Someone else, Elgie insisted, had murdered Aune Newell. He even cast responsibility on the victim when he said that because of her conduct, Aune was bound "to get into some kind of trouble sooner or later," implying that she was too flirtatious with men. Elgie described his client as a man of good character who had tried to help Finland and then joined the RCAF.

McFadden easily disproved Newell's claims as to where he had been at various times on the day of the murder. His cross examination of Elna Lehto, who was a star defence witness, proved that she had perjured herself to protect her lover when she tried to support Newell's lies. McFadden emphasized the evidence against Newell, especially the motivation to rid himself of an inconvenient wife. He described the letter Newell wrote to the woman he had just murdered as a "blind" to throw off the police.

Throughout the trial, Newell made Elgie's job extremely difficult. He frequently shouted at witnesses on the stand. On two occasions he broke away from his guards and tried to assault police detectives who had just testified. Newell sometimes argued openly with his defence counsel. Justice Makins, growing weary of Newell's outbursts, finally asked him, "Did you ever hear the old saying about 'Give a man enough rope...?"

Newell blushed, grinned, and then replied, "Yes, my lord. '... and he'll hang himself.'" However, his antics continued.

On March 15, after deliberating for eleven hours, the jury could not reach a unanimous decision. The jurors voted ten to two for a conviction, and the two holdouts would not be swayed. There would have to be a second trial.

It began on May 5 under the Honourable Mr. Justice Roach. Once again McFadden and Elgie faced each other. This trial dragged on for twenty-five days. Because of Newell's previous bad conduct, he was sometimes removed from the court as a precaution. Nonetheless, he occasionally shouted out that the police were "skunks" and "storm troopers." At one point he even demonstrated feigned disinterest in the trial by reading a Philadelphia newspaper article about a "silk stocking" murder case in the United States. During McFadden's summary, Newell was seen reading passages from the Bible. Once again, the jury was hung. This time the vote was ten to two for acquittal. Elgie had almost won them over with his claim of a police frame-up.

When Newell wasn't in court, he was in Toronto's Don Jail. During the long intervals between trials, he was anything but a model prisoner. He was surly, antagonistic, and foul-mouthed with everybody, even visitors. He once spat on the jail's governor, Walter J. Rayfield, a sixty-year-old First World War hero who had been awarded the Victoria Cross. Newell made one spontaneous attempt to escape, but was quickly caught and subdued.

Newell's constant complaints that he was being mistreated by the guards appeared in the newspapers. This brought about an investigation by the Provincial Inspector of Prisons, T.M. Gourlay. He stated in his report:

> Newell has been about the most difficult prisoner I have known. From the beginning he has deliberately caused trouble and is not satisfied with anything done for him. He has violent fits of temper, and curses everyone … Newell, in my opinion, is solely responsible for any injuries received, and I wish to definitely exonerate all officers concerned from any blame whatever.

Newell made several sham suicide attempts, which were nothing more than publicity stunts. But on one occasion he really did try to kill himself. He tied a large handkerchief to one of his cell bars, and then around his neck. Then he twisted around and around so that he was strangling himself. He almost succeeded before guards saw him and cut him loose. A guard named Joseph Holliday reported:

> His face was a purplish hue, his breathing oozing out in great gulps and very laboured. His chest heaved with the effort, and to all intents he was unconscious. Mr. Rayfield motioned to me to stand by with Mr. Mitchell and wait for Newell to revive … Before we could do anything the prisoner's hands shot to his throat and he attempted to throttle himself by digging his thumbs deeply into his windpipe.

When Newell's hands were forced away, he tried to smash his head against the floor. He cried out hysterically, "Why don't you let me kill myself … I can't spend more months in here." As he was being escorted to the infirmary, Newell became violent and injured two or three guards before he was finally restrained.

Newell even made trouble in his hospital cell, in what he later called a "campaign" to draw public attention to his "inquisition." At night he repeatedly turned the tap in his cell on and off, much to the irritation of the guards and other inmates. He flushed paper drinking cups and wads of tissue down the toilet to block it up. He told Holliday, "If I ever get near one of those fire hose nozzles, I'm going to bash some guard in the head. And it's going to be one of those men who has manhandled me since I've been here."

Gourlay's investigation did not quell the controversy over Newell's allegedly poor treatment in the Don. The men of the Grand Jury were allowed to visit Newell in the jail and have private interviews with him. He told them that he would be thrown in the hole (solitary confinement) for making complaints. This was proven to be utterly false.

However, in those days, Canadian jails still used the strap, a perforated leather belt that inflicted excruciating pain when used to strike a person's naked buttocks. As punishment for his constant bad behaviour, Newell was subjected to six strokes. He took it without a whimper. The paddling only made him more resentful.

On October 6, 1941, one year after Aune's body had been found, Newell's third trial opened before the Honourable Mr. Justice Hope. This time the Crown was represented by T.J. Rigney, K.C. Leading the defence was B.J. Spencer Pitt. Newell had chosen Pitt, a black lawyer, to represent him because, as he explained, he had once had some "negro friends" and liked them. He also said he felt that his previous counsel, Mr. Elgie, had been working with the Crown.

Newell had an outburst on the first day of the trial. Pitt objected to Detective William Mace's presence in the courtroom while other witnesses were giving testimony. Justice Hope ruled that Mace could remain. Newell suddenly shouted that *he* would not allow the trial to proceed as long as Mace was there.

The judge was aware of Newell's behaviour during the previous trials. "I might as well be frank with you," he cautioned, "and let it be understood for the remainder of this trial that you will be dealt with, with entire fairness; but it is not for you to dictate as to how this court should be conducted."

When Newell continued to protest, Hope warned him that he risked being expelled from the courtroom. Newell cried, "I might as well go out now! I will put him out of here!" He leaped over the rail of the prisoner's box, but was subdued before he could get near Mace. He was hauled out of the courtroom. During an intermission, Pitt spoke to him. Newell apologized, and promised to behave himself. He was allowed back in with the warning that if there was any further "unseemly conduct," Newell would be "banished from the court and would remain out of court irrevocably until the conclusion of the trial. I will have no more argument about it."

Rigney had studied the transcripts of the first two trials, and decided to present evidence that had either been understated previously, or overlooked altogether. His first major witness was Orvokki Hakamies. Though she was not fluent in English, Orvokki came across as an intelligent and confident young woman on the witness stand. She had been Aune's confidant in almost everything: financial problems, divorce proceedings, and all matters involving Bill Newell.

Orvokki was asked to explain why she had waited until the evening of the Tuesday after she'd last seen Aune to report her missing. She replied that Newell had suggested that Aune had probably gone to Vineland to visit Billie. She was then asked if she had seen any marks on Newell's face that night.

Orvokki replied that, "he was nervous and would not look at me." If Newell had a scratch on his face, she hadn't seen it because he kept his face in shadows. Newell responded by saying the light was bright enough that night for him to see that Orvokki was wearing too much lipstick. It was a clumsy lie: Orvokki rarely wore makeup at all.

Most of Orvokki's evidence was corroborated by her landlady, Mrs. Ranpors. Furthermore, Annie Kyrojarvi, Aune's aunt with whom Billie was living in Vineland, testified that Aune had been paying her fifteen dollars a month toward the boy's care. She said Aune frequently went to Vineland to see her child. However, in the months that Billie had been with Mrs. Kyrojarvi before Aune's death, Bill had visited his son only once.

In this trial, Elna Lehto was a witness for the Crown. She was Canadian-born, but had been very well-educated in Finland. In addition to English and Finnish, she spoke fluent Swedish and German. She had been infatuated with the dashing Bill Newell, especially when he volunteered to fight for Finland.

Elna had been arrested along with Newell, and then later released on bail. During her time in custody she complained of rough and intimidating treatment at the hands of certain detectives, and even of sexual harassment. These charges of misconduct on the part of some officers had gone a long way to support the accusation of a police frame-up. In the first two trials, Elna lied to protect Newell, partly out of loyalty to him, and partly out of fear. She had not believed that he was guilty of murder.

However, by the time of the third trial, Elna had heard enough to convince her that Newell could indeed be guilty. Her agreement to testify for the Crown was kept secret until the afternoon of October 30, when she was suddenly called to the stand. Newell's face flushed.

Elna testified that she had seen the scratch on Newell's face that fateful night. She said that Bill was "very excited and worried." He told her he'd had an argument with Aune, during which she had scratched him and he had slapped her. That same night, Elna said, Bill had asked her for the first time if she would be a mother to Billie. She also testified that Bill told her the police were accusing him of killing Aune, before the body had even been found.

The Crown presented several letters Newell had written to Elna. In them he expressed his love for her, and his frustration over the difficulties he said Aune was causing him. In one, he complained about having half of his air force pay going to support his wife and child. "I'm not going to do it," he wrote. "I told them [the RCAF] they could discharge me before I'd give Aune anything."

One envelope, posted in Brandon on September 14, 1940, had no letter in it. Elna testified that Newell had destroyed it on the day of his arrest. She told the stunned court that in that letter, Newell had written that he would like to kill Aune.

Letters that Elna had subsequently written to Newell revealed that she rebuked him for such "ugly thoughts." She told him that they could never be happy together, "if you did what you said you would like to." In two letters Newell wrote to Elna after the murder and before his arrest, he made no mention of problems with Aune. Rigney said that was strong evidence that Newell knew she was dead.

One of the main problems for the prosecution had been placing Newell on Centre Island on the day of the murder. They had Constable Agnew's testimony, but that had been clouded by the accusations of a police frame-up. The defence had also established the possibility that the police had tampered with the boots they claimed had dirt from Centre Island on them. However, Rigney turned the case around when he called upon two new witnesses.

Willhelmiina Markhanen was acquainted with both Bill and Aune Newell. She testified that she was in her car at about 2:30 p.m. on September 29, 1940. She had stopped for a red light, and she saw them on Bay Street. They were walking south, toward the ferry docks. She said Aune waved to her and smiled. When asked why she hadn't come forward with this information previously, Willhelmiina replied, "Well, maybe Bill get free and you never know what happened."

Then came Marion Maynes's testimony; her story made her listeners' skin crawl. Mrs. Maynes and her husband Charles had gone canoeing through the Toronto Islands that afternoon. Between 3:30 and four o'clock, they passed through St. Andrew's Cut, which led into the lagoon in which Mugg's Island was located. Charles was on one knee in the back, paddling. He was distracted by water in the bottom of the boat that was soaking his pant leg. Marion was sitting in the middle of the canoe, facing Charles, with her back against the bow thwart. She was looking around, taking in the scenery. The canoe was approaching the southern end of the lagoon, when Marion suddenly caught sight of a woman on the shore to her left. According to Marion's account:

> She was sitting there very still, very quiet … She was staring straight out into space, just sitting staring. And when I first looked at her I thought, Well, I would not want to be sitting on that cold, damp ground. And as I came along in line of her vision her eyes seemed to look directly into mine, and I said to myself, Why, what is the matter? And I stared at her … because something dreadful did seem to be the matter. She had on a black coat and what I took to be a black hat with a brim on it … and the hat seemed to be just jammed on her head without any style or becomingness whatever.
>
> And I stared at her, and somehow had the impression that her face looked bloated. She was very white, and she never moved at all … I felt a strange feeling went through me; I felt if I stared another second I would see something under the surface which was very shadowy and mean, so I looked away. And there was a man in the Air Force uniform standing on the bank fishing … He had just a branch off a tree, a short branch, with a piece of what looked like ordinary cotton string and a hook on the end of it; and he did not know we were on the lagoon until we were there, and he seemed alert all at once; looked at me very sharply as if he thought I might be somebody that knew him; he stared at me, and then he looked at the lady who was sitting on the bank, as if he thought she was making some move or trying to give me a signal of some kind. Then he looked sharply back at me again … and we passed on.

Mrs. Maynes identified Newell as the man she had seen. She said that poor health had prevented her from coming forward earlier. If her story was true, then Newell had just committed the murder when he saw the canoe approaching, and hastily set up a little scene to fool the intruders.

Charles Maynes testified that he had not seen the airman or the girl, but explained that he hadn't looked in that direction. He said that later on his wife had talked to him about it. Pitt said the whole story was a figment of Mrs. Maynes's imagination. Newell scoffed, "I believe she is out of her head."

In an attempt to discredit the testimonies of Markhanen and Maynes, the defence called on three of Newell's friends. They testified that at the time Toots was supposed to be murdering his wife on Centre Island, they saw him in front of Toronto City Hall. These so-called witnesses had obviously been coached in what they were supposed to say. Under cross-examination they became so confused, that their testimony became something of a comic sideshow. One of them said to Rigney, "I don't know nothing about all these questions you keep asking me. All I know is I came here to tell you that that Sunday, September 29th, I saw Newell at a quarter to four."

One new piece of evidence Rigney submitted was the torn envelope that had been found at the murder site. Detectives had gathered up the pieces, re-assembled them, and enclosed the patched-up envelope between glass plates. It was the same sort of YMCA envelope with the RCAF crest that Newell had used for his letters to Elna. At first the investigators could not make sense of the writing and drawing on the envelope, but Elna identified the handwriting as Newell's.

The scribbles and doodles in pencil included *N.S.E.W*., the cardinal points of the compass. The police finally realized that the envelope was a crude topographical map of Centre Island, showing such features as the barbed wire fence surrounding the filtration plant. This became clear when the envelope was compared with aerial photographs of the island. (It was possibly the first time that aerial photography was used in a Canadian murder trial.) Words on the envelope such as "old way no [g]ood" suggested that Newell had used it to plot out an alternative exit route from the murder site, should he not want to go back the way he had come.

One of the most pathetic tales to emerge from the trial was that of Winnifred, Newell's first wife, who had not testified in the first two trials. In the two and a half years of their marriage, Newell had worked only three months. The rest of the time Winnifred and their daughter Doreen subsisted on relief. When Bill demanded a divorce so he could marry Aune, Winnifred refused. So Newell forced her hand by kidnapping Doreen. According to Winnifred's account:

> I would not consent to a divorce, and in June 1937 he came to [her residence] and ran away into the bushes with our twenty-months-old daughter. I did not see the child again until August 1937, when he brought her into Grange Avenue Park for me to see. I made all the requests I was able to to various authorities, including the Children's Aid Society, but I was informed that the only way I could get her was to either take her away as he had done or allow a divorce in the Supreme Court, and in order to get my child I allowed divorce proceedings which I instituted, obtaining my divorce decree *nisi* November 5, 1937, and degree absolute was granted six months later. My married life was upset by the usual family quarrels, but I will say that my husband has a very violent temper when agitated to a point.

Winnifred's father paid for the divorce. Newell ignored requests to pay for the child's support. Winnifred did not see her ex-husband again until she was obliged to go to court to testify against him. Amazingly, she held Aune responsible for all of her troubles.

The situation looked bad for Newell, and it got worse when he took the stand to testify in his own defence. He was belligerent, and just as evasive in answering his own counsel's questions as he was with those of the prosecution. He lied and he often contradicted himself. At times, the sheer lack of basic logic in his explanations bewildered everyone in the courtroom.

Newell denied the evidence given by his own divorce lawyer and RCAF officers that he wanted support payments to go to Elna instead of Aune. Asked whether or not a supposed divorce/support agreement he had reached with Aune was definite, he replied, "When I say it was not definite, it was definite to an extent only in so much as either one could change our mind without consulting the other."

Later he elaborated on the alleged agreement with Aune. "But when a divorce went through, we could still live together maybe, because I told her I would kick Elna out and go back, because blood is thicker than water, and I would have given up Elna anytime for to have Billie back."

Newell said that when he had lunch with Aune that Sunday afternoon, she ate some meat, onions, and apple pie. That was not at all consistent with the findings of the *post mortem*, in which the contents of the stomach had been examined. Newell also claimed that he had been supporting his son, but Elna had made him stop the payments.

On the witness stand, Newell persisted with his claim that the police were out to frame him. He denied giving statements to Detective Skinner or any other officer. Strands of fabric that the police had found caught on twigs at the murder site matched the material of Newell's uniform pants. He said that the police had planted them after taking his clothes while he was in the Don Jail. He said the same thing had happened with those incriminating pieces of torn envelope.

Newell frequently uttered wisecracks and sarcastic remarks to smear the Crown witnesses. Of himself, he said, "I may be a heel in some ways and tell a lot of lies, when I am not on this stand, to two or three different women, or something, but I never did that [murder] to anybody in my life … if this jury met me outside they would go home and tell their wives they met a nice fellow from the Air Force."

After seven long weeks of testimony, Justice Hope gave his instructions to the jury on November 22. The twelve men deliberated for over five hours before reaching a unanimous decision. They found the "nice fellow from the Air Force" guilty of murder.

Asked by Justice Hope if he had anything to say before sentence was passed, Newell replied, "I did not expect a fair trial; I never have since it started … The jury, I believe, are decent, upright citizens. You led them away with your talk." Hope sentenced Newell to be hanged on February 12, 1942.

Pitt's appeal to the Supreme Court of Ontario was turned down, as was his application for clemency to the federal Ministry of Justice. Newell had converted to Roman Catholicism, and his spiritual advisor, Father C.W. James, submitted his own plea to have the death sentence commuted. That also failed.

In his last hours Newell wrote a letter to Pitt in which he thanked the lawyer for his efforts. "Against tremendous odds you put up a remarkable fight and even though the verdict was against us still you cannot be blamed for that ... The fault was with the Crown only who suppressed certain facts and accepted perjured testimony."

On the morning of the execution, Newell insisted on wearing a new shirt and tie. He refused a sedative, and walked stoically from the death cell to the gallows. The only witnesses to the hanging were the unidentified executioner, the County Sheriff, the Governor of the jail, the jail physician, Father James, and two guards.

With the black hood over his head and the rope around his neck, Newell allegedly said, "I am innocent," the moment before the hangman sprang the trap. It was not a clean execution. Newell's neck was not broken by the drop, and he slowly strangled. Later, there was a story that the guards pulled on his legs to hasten an end to his ordeal. Newell hung for thirty-five minutes before the physician pronounced him dead. His body was released to his family and buried in Mount Hope Cemetery.

An unsubstantiated rumour said that Newell confessed to the crime before taking the final walk. There were also whispers that he was the real victim. While some RCAF officers had described Newell as unscrupulous and deceitful, several of his fellow airmen had spoken in his defence. With Canada embroiled in the war against Nazi Germany, the public tended to be sympathetic toward young enlisted men who got in trouble. Policemen who were not in the armed forces were often labelled "slackers," even though they were doing an essential job at home. It wasn't too great a leap for the public to believe they would frame an innocent man in order to close the books on a capital crime. Moreover, the women with whom Newell had become involved were "foreigners," and therefore worthy of suspicion.

For many years after the tragic events of 1940–41, the spot where Aune "Spooky" Newell's body had been found was known in Toronto lore as Murderer's Island. A children's legend arose that the killer had hidden loot — a silver watch, ring, and brooch — in the lagoon. Adventurous boys dove in search of these prizes before the area was eventually taken over by a marina. The Newell tragedy was soon pushed out of the public consciousness by the greater drama of the war. Toronto's Silk Stocking Murder is now a largely forgotten story.

# BIBLIOGRAPHY

## BOOKS

Anderson, Frank W. *The Vernon Booher Murder Case*. Saskatoon: Gopher Books, 1979.

Boyd, Neil. *The Last Dance: Murder in Canada*. Scarborough, ON: Prentice-Hall Canada, 1988.

Burkholder, Ruth. *Burkholders With Roots in Ontario*. Stouffville, ON: RME Services, 1993.

Firth, Edith, G. (ed). *The Town of York: 1793 – 1815*. Toronto: University of Toronto Press, 1962.

Fitzgerald, Jack. *Ten Steps to the Gallows*. St. John's, NL: Creative Publishers, 2006.

Fulford, Roger. *Royal Dukes: The Father and Uncles of Queen Victoria*. London, UK: Collins, 1973.

Gillen, Mollie, *The Prince and His Lady*. Griffen House, Toronto, 1970.

Guillet, Edwin C. *The Walk and the Kiss*. Richmond Hill, ON: Simon & Schuster, 1973.

Hounsom, Eric Wilfrid. *Toronto in 1810*. Toronto: Ryerson Press, 1970.

Jenkins, McKay. *Bloody Falls of the Coppermine*. New York: Random House, 2006.

Kennedy, Ian. *Sunny, Sandy, Savary*. Comox, BC: Kennell Publishing, 1992.

Moyles, R.G. *British Law and Arctic Men*. Saskatoon: Western Producer Prairie Books, 1979.

Newton, David. *Tainted Justice*. Sydney, NS: University College of Cape Breton Press, 1995.

Pfeifer, Jeffrey and Ken Leyton Brown. *Death by Rope, Vol. 1: 1867 –1923*. Regina: Centax Books, 2007.

Pflug, Sgt. Douglas (ed). *Fingerprints Through Time: A History of the Guelph Police*. Guelph, ON: Log Cabin Press, 2009.

Reaman, G. Elmore. *A History of Vaughan Township*. Toronto: University of Toronto Press, 1971.

Robertson, J. Ross. *Robertson's Landmarks of Toronto, Vol. 5*. Toronto: Toronto *Evening Telegram*, 1908.

Robin, Martin. *The Bad and the Lonely*. Toronto: James Lorimer & Company, 1976.

Wallace, W. Stewart. *Murders and Mysteries*. Toronto: MacMillan and Company, 1931.

## PERIODICALS

Breese, Kim. "The Harvey Murders." *Guelph Historical Society*, Vol. XLII, 2003.

Irwin, Ross W. "Capital Punishment in Wellington County." *Wellington County Historical Society*, Vol. XV, 2002.

## NEWSPAPERS

The *Edmonton Journal*

The *Guelph Mercury*

The *Halifax Herald*

The *Hamilton Herald*

The *Hamilton Spectator*

The *Mannville News*

The *St. John's Newfoundlander*

The *Sydney Daily Post*

The *Toronto Globe*

The *Globe & Mail*

The *Toronto Star*

The *Victoria Daily Colonist*

The *York Gazette*

## MISCELLANEOUS

Letters by John Paul Radelmüller. Upper Canada Sundries, National Archives of Canada

# ALSO BY EDWARD BUTTS

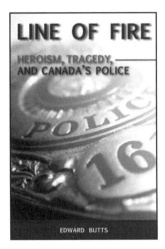

**LINE OF FIRE**
**Heroism, Tragedy, and Canada's Police**
978-1554883912
$24.99

Across Canada peace officers put their lives on the line every day. From John Fisk in 1804, the first known Canadian policeman killed in the line of duty, to the four RCMP officers shot to death in Mayerthorpe, Alberta, in 2005, Edward Butts takes a hard-hitting, compassionate, probing look at some of the stories involving the hundreds of Canadian law-enforcement officers who have found themselves in harm's way. One thing is certain about all of these peace officers: they displayed amazing courage and never hesitated to make the ultimate sacrifice for their fellow citizens.

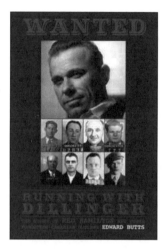

**RUNNING WITH DILLINGER**
**The Story of Red Hamilton and Other Forgotten Canadian Outlaws**
978-155002832
$24.99

This book picks up where *The Desperate Ones: Canada's Forgotten Outlaws* left off. Here are more remarkable true stories about Canadian crimes and criminals — most of them tales that have been buried for years. The stories begin in colonial Newfoundland, with robbery and murder committed by the notorious Power Gang. As readers travel across the country and through time, they will meet the last two men to be hanged in Prince Edward Island, smugglers who made lake Champlain a battleground, and teenage girls who committed murder in their escape from jail. They will meet the bandits who plundered banks and trains. Among them were Sam Behan, a robber whose harrowing testimony about the brutal conditions in the Kingston Penitentiary may have brought about his untimely death in "The Hole"; and John "Red" Hamilton, the Canadian-born member of the legendary Dillinger gang.

**Marquis Book Printing Inc.**

Québec, Canada
2011